MR & MRS SMITH PRESENTS

THE WORLD'S SEXIEST BEDROOMS

MR & MRS SMITH PRESENTS

THE
WORLD'S
SEXIEST
BEDROOMS

WITH OVER 200 ILLUSTRATIONS
PHOTOGRAPHS BY POLLY BROWN

TEXT BY SARAH JAPPY

Thames & Hudson

CONTENTS

EXPERIENCED IN THE BEDROOM

We'll let you in on a little secret … Even after 15 years of hotel-hopping, we *still* get that little thrill when we know we've got a new bedroom all to ourselves. We still make a break for the bathroom to browse the products, we do a quick stock-take of the minibar, and we sure as hell still swan-dive onto the bed. (We couldn't possibly admit to any chandelier-swinging, though …)

And so, in celebration of the very special bedrooms that have seduced us over the years, we present to you this book: a collection of date-night favourites and head-turning new passions from around the world. Be it city-surveying crashpads, desert-island hideaways or treetop jungle perches that get you in the mood, we know just the place, shot in full come-hither glory by photographer Polly Brown.

Think of it as your ultimate hotel 'to do' list: a unique array of the wildly romantic and the downright sexy; the richly coloured, the elegantly designed, the perfectly panorama'd; the ones with private terraces, private pools, private beaches …

Not that we neglect the bathrooms, mind. Twin tubs, tubs for two, a hot-tub terrace, showers that could fit a sports team (if you so wish) – they all get big ticks here. And if you manage to remove that DO NOT DISTURB sign from the door, we'll point you to some other handpicked hotel highlights: cosy lounges, candlelit corners and spas that scream indulgence.

Finally, you'll find a few ideas that we had in our first guide book all those years ago (and still have on our website today); those things truly Worth Getting Out Of Bed For, should you feel like a little local adventure. Oh, and a few choice words from our under-covers crew of reviewers, too: the well-travelled tastemakers (and their partners) we trust to double-check each and every stay.

So this is a book for all you hopeless romantics, whether you're out to woo on a weekend away, planning *the* honeymoon or just thinking: 'I'm smitten. Get me there immediately …'

Suite dreams,

Smith

Mr & Mrs Smith

VENICE ITALY

La Serenissima's liquid lures form a formidable part of the city's seduction, but there's plenty here for landlubbers, too: Byzantine, Renaissance and Baroque architectural showstoppers at every turn, plus a holiday's worth of *palazzi*, *piazze* and antipasti.

Snapped while the locals lingered over spaghetti alle vongole

Aman Venice

ITALY

STYLE BAROQUE 'N' ROLL
SETTING GRAND CANAL PERCH

Housed inside the Palazzo Papadopoli (built for Bergamo aristocracy, then sold to the Papadopoli clan: Venetian mega-merchants), Aman Venice has always been something of a trailblazer – literally: it was the first building in Venice to get electric lights. Other dazzling flourishes include frescoed ceilings, gilded flourishes and gold a-go-go. Despite its 600-odd birthdays, it shows no signs of slowing down; George and Amal picked it as the venue for their wedding celebrations, after all. You could easily contract a particular type of mania here ('Aman-ia', if you will), in which you mistakenly believe that you, too, are an off-duty A-lister. Items that will have you thus deluded include: the jet-set airport transfer in the hotel's custom-made, royal-standard boat, the secret jetty entrance, the paparazzi-proof garden and that decadent decor.

'This is luxury on another level. Communal rooms inspire a litany of superlatives (opulent, ornate, decadent), the fireplaces are enormous, the pianos grand, the built-in bookcases the sort of thing Casanova might have organized.'

JAMES LOHAN, THE ORIGINAL MR SMITH

THE FINER DETAILS

BEDTIME

Alcova Tiepolo Suite The ceiling is a blaze of glory, decorated with a fresco by 18th-century painter Giovanni Battista Tiepolo (whose family once owned the palazzo). Continuing the celestial theme, there's an elegant sitting room decorated with gilded stucco reliefs and chinoiserie fabric, plus a swish modern bathroom, home to a *doge-worthy* bathtub and separate shower. Tech-touches include a Bang & Olufsen flatscreen TV and DVD player, and a pre-loaded iPod and dock. A beach bag, sun hat and adaptor plug count among the thoughtful extras.

WORTH GETTING OUT OF BED FOR

Resistance is futile: tick off the tourist essentials by sipping a bellini at Harry's Bar, cruising the canals in a gondola and marvelling at the Doge's Palace. Pay your respects to Titian, who sleeps the eternal sleep in the nearby 14th-century Basilica dei Frari; two of his works still hang there. Sculpture-clad San Rocco is a Baroque beauty with gilded ceilings; Tintoretto's brushwork adorns the Scuola Grande di San Rocco. Gasp at San Giacomo di Rialto's Gothic portico, a five-minute walk from the hotel; playwright Carlo Goldoni's house, a 10-minute walk away, has a veritable stash of theatrical artefacts. Hop in a water taxi to watch flamboyantly skilful glassblowing on the island of Murano, before exploring the glittering showrooms. In January and February, catch the pageantry of Carnevale (pick up masks from Ca' Macana, the shop that kitted out Tom Cruise and co in *Eyes Wide Shut*). The modern-art maelstrom that is the Venice Biennale kicks off in May (during odd-numbered years). Back at Aman, retreat to the terrace for *la dolce vita* views, or head to the Asian-influenced spa for treatments.

FOOD AND DRINK

Aman's Arva restaurant is the fruit of chef Dario Ossola's labours. His menu champions hospitality and simplicity, refined with cheffy tricks and wizard techniques. What's on offer flexes with the seasons; highlights have included chestnut tagliatelle, chanterelles and Castelmagno cheese, and baked guinea fowl with parsnips and black garlic. The dining rooms up the ante, whether you settle in the canal-spying, fresco-finessed Yellow Room or the equally ravishing Red Room, which overlooks the gardens and comes with shimmering Murano chandeliers. After dinner, retire to the bar and order slender flutes of prosecco, sit by the crackling fire and toast the good decisions that have brought you here.

DRESS CODE

Honour your spectacular setting with garments worthy of Titian and jewels fit for Giorgione.

'After dinner, retire to the bar and order flutes of prosecco, sit by the crackling fire and toast the good decisions that have brought you here.'

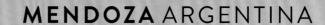

MENDOZA ARGENTINA

Raise a glass to mountainous Mendoza, which lies at the handsome heart of Argentina's wine country. This picturesque province knows a thing or two about bacchanalian refreshments, but beyond the vineyards and foothills, Art Deco architecture and gracious squares await.

Shot during March's sun-dappled wine harvest

Casa de Uco

MENDOZA, ARGENTINA

STYLE ARCHITECTURALLY INTOXICATING
SETTING MIGHTY VINE SURROUNDINGS

According to French microbiologist and chemist Louis Pasteur, wine is the 'most healthful and most hygienic of beverages'. That basically makes Casa de Uco, a magnificent wine estate set in the resplendent Uco Valley, a doctor-approved choice. This adventure-loving hotel's green fingers extend beyond its rows of verdant vines; the organic vegetable garden provides for the excellent restaurant, and home-grown ingredients feature in the Argentine spa treatments. The Casa is mighty good-looking, too, in an unapologetically industrial way: an architectural dialogue involving glass and steel that deliberately clashes with its ravishingly rural backdrop. There are valleys, vineyards and mountains to explore if you so wish; a minimalist spa, sauna, steam room, gym, stables, tennis courts, games room and lagoon-view infinity pool to enjoy if you don't.

'I thought about taking a bottle (and, as an afterthought, Mr Smith) to the Andes-ogling Jacuzzi – for why was the romantic mini-break invented, if not to revel in every amorous cliché under the sun?'

LUCINDA PAXTON, NOMADIC SCRIBE

THE FINER DETAILS

BEDTIME

One-bedroom Villa You'll need to skip outside to enjoy the villa's very best bit: a private rooftop pool with grin-inducing views of the grapevines, the Andes mountains and the Cordón del Plata. Keeping the focus al fresco, the villa also has a fire pit, an interior courtyard and a seating area with floor-to-ceiling glass walls, so you can continue to eye up the valley and the surrounding frosted peaks. Interiors are styled with Corbusier-esque clean-cut modernism; warm-hued wood, textured fabrics and sunny pops of colour keep things cosy.

WORTH GETTING OUT OF BED FOR

Grape things await holidaying oenophiles here: the region has a veritable surfeit of vineyards. Malbec and sémillon are the acknowledged headline acts, but the region's diverse *terroir* also yields noteworthy chardonnay, sauvignon blanc and pinot noir. Swot up at the Vines of Mendoza winery; you'll get a delicious education in their fermentation process, sample ambrosial nectars from the barrels and even blend your own. Explore the estate on bicycles or hop on horses, accompanied by a trusty guide (and a hotel-prepped picnic). If your lust for adventure extends further afield, you could embark on a hiking expedition deep into the Andean hills.

FOOD AND DRINK

When expert farmers are your near neighbours, it's sensible to make the most of them. Casa de Uco does exactly that: its resident chefs source the very best local meat, fish and produce from the suppliers that share their patch of paradise. Sun-ripened vegetables are plucked from the fertile soil of the organic garden. The restaurant's menu pays loving tribute to the Uco Valley's natural larder: dishes such as breaded trout with roasted pumpkin and carrots, rocket and spiced yogurt, for example. Carnivores will enjoy the meat-tastic *asados* held in the vineyard.

DRESS CODE

Gaucho-on-payday: model silks, leather and wools, malbec-red accents and glints of gold. NB: Avoid white jodhpurs and blue shirts, unless you relish being mistaken for staff.

'Good-looking in an unapologetically industrial way: an architectural dialogue involving glass and steel that deliberately clashes with its ravishingly rural backdrop.'

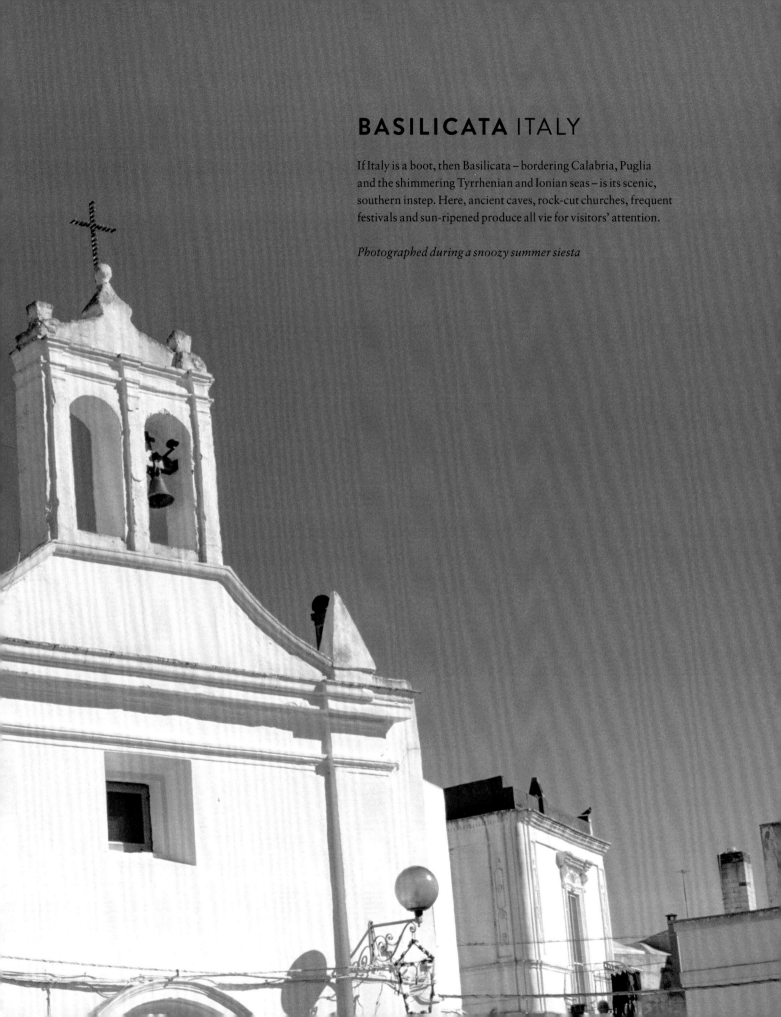

BASILICATA ITALY

If Italy is a boot, then Basilicata – bordering Calabria, Puglia and the shimmering Tyrrhenian and Ionian seas – is its scenic, southern instep. Here, ancient caves, rock-cut churches, frequent festivals and sun-ripened produce all vie for visitors' attention.

Photographed during a snoozy summer siesta

Palazzo Margherita

BASILICATA, ITALY

STYLE DIRECTED BY COPPOLA
SETTING CINEMATIC BERNALDA

In a roundabout way, we have Francis Ford Coppola's grandfather to thank for Palazzo Margherita. *Nonno* Coppola hailed from the small southern Italian town of Bernalda in Matera, and it was while exploring the historic region that his famous grandson first encountered this then-crumbling palazzo. Spotting its potential, canny Francis lavished love, time and attention on its transformation, used it as a wedding venue for his daughter Sophia's nuptials in 2004, and turned it into a luxury hotel. Movie-makers should clearly turn their hands to boutique bedrooms more often. Palazzo Margherita's box office-smash attractions include suites styled with Don-worthy decadence, romantic gardens with a peaceful pool, rustic home-cooking, charming staff and a trio of bars. It goes without saying that there's also an opulent screening room – plus Francis FC's personal film collection, for guests to dip into.

'We sashay downstairs for a perambulation
in the formal gardens. They are breathtakingly
beautiful, with palms, fragrant climbers,
a fountain and a long, covered pergola –
it's an undeniably romantic setting.'

FAYE TOOGOOD, DESIGN DOYENNE

THE FINER DETAILS

BEDTIME

Suite Nine Forget the director's seat – this is the director's suite: Coppola's preferred sleeping quarters, which he designed himself in honour of his Tunisian grandmother (hence the bold, teal herringbone *bejmat*-tiled floor and kaleidoscopic ceiling). No doubt his grandma would approve of the garden-spying, fully furnished terrace and the suite's Art Deco-style black-and-tangerine fireplace. The bathroom is no shrinking violet: it's decorated in colour-pop patterned tiles and white marble, with a roll-top bathtub and a separate shower. Sit and pen your Coppola-worthy script at the large Italianate writing desk, facing the three arched windows.

WORTH GETTING OUT OF BED FOR

Take free cookery classes with the resident chefs: you'll go home armed with *nonna*-worthy tomato sauce-making skills. Potter around Bernalda, a petite and peaceful medieval commune with a few frescoed churches, a smattering of historic monuments and a castle. Hop in your car for the 40-minute drive to Matera, which has starred in several films, largely thanks to the incredible Sassi di Matera and their prehistoric cave dwellings. The Musma (museum of contemporary sculpture), housed in a decaying palazzo, offers a dramatic backdrop to the art displayed within. Beach bunnies can adjourn to the seashore, where suitable-for-sunbathing areas are dotted along the Ionian coast; the hotel can sort access to beach clubs on the Marina di Pisticci's pale sands. Request a private film screening for two in the Salon, whose design was inspired by neo-realist maestro Luchino Visconti.

FOOD AND DRINK

Palazzo Margherita nails that relaxed-but-ravishing approach to food that Italians have made entirely their own. There's no formal restaurant; instead, guests are invited to dine in the kitchen or in the courtyard. Dishes such as sausage with rocket and grilled pork rib over-deliver on their bashful billing. Breakfast is similarly simple: an utterly unpretentious spread of pastries, fresh fruit, cheese and charcuterie, plus plenty of excellent Italian coffee. You have three places to slake your thirst (this is the land of the world-famous Basilicata wine, after all): one poolside, one with pizza and town-square views, and lastly the formal Family Bar, styled with Le Manach fabric-clad walls, the palazzo's original chandelier and a vintage bar from Turin.

DRESS CODE

Don Corleone gone a-courting: crisp white shirts, cashmere and Italian shoes for the Mr; siren-sexy frocks and arched Italianate eyebrows for the Mrs.

'Forget the director's seat – this is the director's suite: Coppola's preferred sleeping quarters, which he designed himself in honour of his Tunisian grandmother.'

PHUKET THAILAND

Patong, Phuket's lively main resort town, may draw nightlife-loving visitors, but that doesn't mean you have to join them. Instead, investigate the island's lesser-populated lures: rugged rainforests, lofty mountains and bright-white stretches of sand.

Photographed in between monsoon soakings

Keemala

PHUKET, THAILAND

STYLE PEACE IN A POD
SETTING TRANQUIL TROPICAL WOODLAND

According to Dorothy, there's no place like home. According to this hotel's lucky guests, there's no place like Keemala. Here, sleeping quarters riff dreamily on the imagined dwellings of mythical Thai tribes: pick from tented hideaways, clay cottages, leaf-laced treehouses and cloud-poking 'bird's nests', all orchestrated with architectural wizardry. Communal areas and a spectacular spa are housed in pods and thatched hobbit-holes, scattered like giant seeds in the evergreen wilderness. Phuket has ten-a-penny beachfront boltholes; unconventional Keemala embraces its woodland setting, encouraging guests to swap sandside somnolence for local adventures: flit to villages, monasteries, elephant sanctuaries and secret islands.

'Mr Smith, who finds it very hard to sit still, proclaimed one morning that "This is the most relaxed state I have ever been in," and on our last day, quietly said, "Please don't make me leave."'

SOPHIE MICHELL, MS MASTERCHEF

THE FINER DETAILS

BEDTIME

Bird's Nest Pool Villa If our birds' nests looked anything like Keemala's, we wouldn't be flying the coop anytime soon. Inspired by an intriguing mix of history and myth, each of the eight treetop Bird's Nest Pool Villas is a cocoon of woven wood and shapely steel, with a glass wall overlooking lush rainforest, rugged mountains and the glittering Andaman Sea. Forget romancing the stone – romance the four-poster bed, the al fresco bathtub or the private lap pool, instead. Bonus points go to the huge leather-chest minibars, sea-surveying showers, traditional coffee-grinders (and beans from Chiang Rai) and expert villa hosts.

WORTH GETTING OUT OF BED FOR

Your brilliant villa host can arrange a flock of adventures: discover local islands and hidden beaches; go snorkelling with manta rays and leopard sharks; at Phuket's sanctuary, spy on elephants in their rainforest retirement home. Back at boutique basecamp, there's a bunch of free fitness classes to try, from meditation and yoga to Thai boxing and tai chi. Conscientious Keemala organizes a monthly beach clean-up; join in if you can. Be tapped with wooden sticks (trust us, it works) at the incredible spa, which has a meditation cave and treatment rooms set in thatched huts. The on-site culinary academy will school you in the art of *gaeng phed goong* (red curry with prawns) or *kluoy buad chi* (bananas in coconut syrup) and let you pick your own organic ingredients. Or try zorbing and ziplining through Kathu forest, boat trips to pretty beaches or alms-giving expeditions to local monasteries. You'll want to meet the hotel's resident pair of water buffalo (plus the chicken, peacocks, ducks and goats), too.

FOOD AND DRINK

Food is a proud feather in Keemala's cap. Eat your way across an ancient spice route without moving a muscle (just your jaw) at Mala, where the menu hops from southern Thailand to India, China to Sri Lanka. The hotel puts a new spin on magic mushrooms: its fat fungi, served in the restaurant, are plucked from the hotel's 'enchanted' garden. Book one of the dinky private-dining pods: two-person hidey-holes clustered around the peaceful pool. A burbling waterfall obligingly sets the scene. Cha-La Pool Bar serves light meals and strong cocktails: highlights include a lime and lemongrass-infused *tom yum* number, and a Wonka-worthy bittersweet martini starring raw cacao. Don't miss Keemala's take on afternoon tea, served with samosas and pâtisserie with tropical inflections. Further afield, visit the night market in Kamala for spicy noodles, fried-fish skewers and banana pancakes with condensed milk.

DRESS CODE

Fly guy/girl: flaunt your best plumage.

'Inspired by an intriguing mix of history and myth, each of the eight treetop Bird's Nest Pool Villas is a cocoon of woven wood and shapely steel.'

BERKSHIRE UK

In bucolic Berkshire, just a Thames-tootle from London, queens have royal residences (hello, Windsor Castle) and fictional toads have halls. While the local animals don't actually talk or drive, the landscapes really are as pretty as *The Wind in the Willows* would have you believe.

Captured as the conkers dropped

Cliveden

BERKSHIRE, UK

STYLE NEOCLASSICAL 'N' NAUGHTY
SETTING BUCOLIC BERKSHIRE

Cliveden's seduction begins before the bedroom: its metaphorical striptease starts as your car purrs down that rolling drive towards the Italianate mansion that awaits. As scandalous pasts go, Cliveden's takes some beating: the estate was built as a love-gift for the Duke of Buckingham's mistress, the Countess of Shrewsbury (her enraged husband challenged Buckingham to a duel – losing his life in the process). Fast-forward a few centuries and the walled garden is where John Profumo first clapped eyes on Christine Keeler, as she put the swimming pool to the test. (It passed with flying colours, if the politician and showgirl's infamous ensuing affair is anything to go by.) Have your own dissolute-or-otherwise romance at this magnificent manor, which has an aristocratic fun side: cue a snooker room, tennis courts, a boathouse with three boats, and a helipad. Added charms include a chandeliered, portrait-lined restaurant and a whisper-quiet spa with two al fresco hot tubs, set in rose- and lavender-lavished gardens.

'The long, wide drive allows the view to sink in slowly and the horseshoe-shaped Italianate mansion at its end is breathtakingly beautiful, way beyond grand. Frankly, we are no longer Mr and Mrs Smith, we've just been made Lord and Lady.'

JAKE KNOWLES, INTREPID ADVERTISER

THE FINER DETAILS

BEDTIME

Prince of Wales Suite Judging by his eponymous suite, Prince Frederick (an 18th-century Prince of Wales) knew a thing or two about romancing. This is no time to play the shrinking violet: take your cue from the suite's passion-red living room and king-size bed, swathed in heavy, emerald-green fabric. The drama continues in the opulent en-suite bathroom, festooned with dark-red frescoes. Regency-style furnishings, an ornate fireplace and traditional artworks up the ante even further. If you can tear your eyes away from each other and the regal decor, the suite overlooks the parterre gardens, where you just might spy a tabloid-worthy scandal unfolding.

WORTH GETTING OUT OF BED FOR

Cliveden has a mini-flotilla of boats, so take to the river with your sweetheart (champagne, strawberries and a straw hat tipped at a rakish angle: highly recommended). Indulge in a pampering session at the spa, where treatments commence with a footbath and a chinwag with a therapist about your needs. If the thought of cream-slathered scones makes your pulse quicken, don't miss afternoon tea in the Great Hall, which earns its name – and then some. Head to the pool: scene of historic *liaisons dangereuses*. Increase the likelihood of your own poolside Profumo moment by bringing your most come-hither swimwear. (When not swimming naked – as she was here – Christine favoured a natty striped one-piece.)

FOOD AND DRINK

The birthplace of the £100 club sandwich has more than costly carbs up its sleeve. At the restaurant, Michelin-starred chef André Garrett runs the show, delighting diners with dishes fit for the landed gentry: wild sea trout with Cornish mussels and St George mushrooms, or fallow deer with salt-baked celeriac, for example. The setting gives the food a run for its money: all glittering chandeliers, portrait-lined walls, white linen and plush, crushed velvet in boiled-sweet hues. Enjoy brunch, afternoon tea and best-of-British gastro-offerings in what was once Lord Astor's stable block; for champagne cocktails served in splendour, head to the Great Hall (keeping an eye on the stonking staircase to see who's coming down it).

DRESS CODE

If in doubt, ask yourself: what would Winston (Churchill) do? Accessorize with a cigar, to puff on contemplatively on the terrace.

'This is no time to play the shrinking violet: take your cue from the suite's passion-red living room and king-size bed, swathed in heavy, emerald-green fabric.'

NHA TRANG VIETNAM

This vibrant resort may know how to party (buzzing bars are scattered like seashells across the beachfront), but its best bits are quieter: uninterrupted stretches of white sand, emerald-aqua waters, tropical islands and world-class diving, for starters.

Photographed on a perfect-for-diving day in February

Six Senses Ninh Van Bay

NHA TRANG, VIETNAM

STYLE BAY WATCH

SETTING TROPICAL TREAT

Where a white-sand beach meets the towering mountains, lush jungle and the East Vietnam Sea, you'll find Six Senses Ninh Van Bay – well, once you've hopped on the hotel's private boat to get there, that is. This remote getaway has a flotilla of VIP villas, an army of attentive butlers and a fleet of nimble-knuckled masseuses and therapists. There's a quiet communal pool, but most guests loll about in their private one or in the sea, only returning to dry land for generous helpings of seafood hot pot and *banh xeo* (stuffed savoury pancakes) at the restaurants, or indulgent treatments at the world-famous spa. If you want to bump into anyone other than your fellow guests, local fishermen will take you out onto the waters.

'The window overlooking our own infinity pool and the beach beyond is most impressive, although Mr Smith is having problems dragging himself away from another arresting sight: the champagne-stocked fridge.'

CARRIE KWAN, ON-THE-PULSE BLOGGER

THE FINER DETAILS

BEDTIME

Rock Pool Villa This thatched villa-on-stilts is nestled into boulders the size of a giant's football, within diving reach of the sea. It's tucked away on the secluded western area of the bay, accessed via a scenic hilltop staircase. Items you're unlikely to have back home include: a handcrafted wooden bathtub and the sea-surveying deck with private plunge pool; there's also an al fresco shower. Toffee-hued wood dominates the villa's interior, which glows like golden syrup when the sun shines (often).

WORTH GETTING OUT OF BED FOR

Make the most of the resort's LIFE (leisure/interest/fun/entertainment) centre: tackle the waters by water ski or catamaran, or duck below the surface for snorkelling or diving. You could also island-hop by boat or visit a lobster farm. Early birds catch the fish – so skip snoozing and spend the morning with the friendly local fishermen, who will take you out on their boats, and show you how to prep the nets and lure in the glittering catch. Landlubbers could chase waterfalls, embark on hilltop hikes to hidden coves or try a cookery class. Indulge in the spa's Vietnamese Wellness Journey: a traditional bamboo massage with suction cups, a reiki crystal facial and plentiful servings of fresh fruit, vegetarian handrolls and tea from the organic garden. Don't miss the twice-weekly starlight cinema at Drinks by the Beach bar; you could catch a classic or a new release, viewed in a setting that's sure to make your local silver screen look a little lacklustre.

FOOD AND DRINK

The hotel gets its toothsome fresh organic produce from the temperate region of Dalat, which is three hours away; the fattest, most flavoursome seafood (juicy king prawns, succulent lobster) is plucked from the waves by the expert fishermen. (Request an in-villa barbecue to enjoy their catch.) Six Senses has a trio of restaurants: the view-toting, open-all-day Dining by the Bay; the relaxed Dining by the Pool (ideal for light lunches); and fancy-pants Dining by the Rocks, which occupies a vertiginous clifftop perch. The hotel doesn't hold back when it comes to liquid thrills: the thatch-tastic Drinks by the Beach serves up sunset views of the sea and the peaks from its central sandside vantage point.

DRESS CODE

The jungle look: splashes of emerald, loose shirts and Mowgli-tousled hair.

'Guests loll about in their private pool or in the sea, only returning to dry land for generous helpings of seafood hot pot and *banh xeo*.'

TUSCANY ITALY

Fields, vineyards and the occasional cloud unfurl in dramatic splendour across Tuscany's bucolic landscapes, which span countryside and coast, yielding world-class wine, olive oil – and mellow Monteverdi.

Shot when the olives were ripe for the picking

Monteverdi

TUSCANY, ITALY

STYLE VILLAGE PEOPLE
SETTING CALMING CASTIGLIONCELLO

Italians really *do* do it better. Case in point: mellow Monteverdi, a hilltop hideaway surrounded by emerald, gold and russet fields. This former medieval village in the heart of Italy's world-class winelands counts a lavender-fringed infinity pool, an exceptionally clever chef and a perfumed spa among its charms; its take on *la dolce vita* feels deliciously authentic. As if all that wasn't typically Tuscan enough, there are also the ruins of a 12th-century castle – discovered by Monteverdi's enterprising owner – to explore.

'We head back to our hilltop bubble for an afternoon swim *à deux*, a shower in our cool room, aperitivos and dinner. *Perfetto*. Whoever said you can't buy class clearly had never stayed at Monteverdi.'

JESS CARTNER-MORLEY, FRONT-ROW FASHIONISTA

THE FINER DETAILS

BEDTIME

Luxury View Suite Forget bedtime, it's bathtime – in this Val d'Orcia-spying, heart-flutteringly romantic suite, at least. Its chief attraction (in addition to the peaceful decor, chunky exposed beams, agricultural ephemera and Tuscan-panorama windows) is the bold, black bathtub, positioned meaningfully at the centre of the bedroom. Pretty flowers from the hotel gardens and paintings by local artists add smatterings of colour to the pale, poised palette.

WORTH GETTING OUT OF BED FOR

This is the time and place to while away hours in dreamy pastoral pursuits: sketching in the lavender garden; wine, olive oil and cheese tastings at the local *enoteca*; or gentle discussions with the current artist-in-residence. Monteverdi is a *gnocco*'s throw from some of the prettiest towns in Italy: Montepulciano – a treasure trove of restaurants, frescoed churches and winding streets lined with *gelaterias* and *enotecas* – is a 30-minute drive away; Sarteano is the perfect size for a shady, atmospheric wander from piazza to hilltop *fortezza*. You could also hop to La Foce's fabulous gardens, 15 minutes away by car. Grape-lovers should seek out Vino Nobile (one of Italy's hero reds) among Montepulciano's vineyards, or spicy, juicy Brunello at Montalcino. Learn how to make *pici* pasta and wild-boar ragù with the help of the hotel's handy chefs. If the thought of cooking up a storm doesn't get you going, opt for a romantic ritual or two at the spa, where the rubs and scrubs rely on fragrant unguents sourced from the famous 13th-century Florentine *farmacia*, Santa Maria Novella.

FOOD AND DRINK

Round these parts, life centres around the *cucina*. Thankfully, Monteverdi has two ridiculously tasty restaurants to settle into, each one delivering *nonna*-worthy Tuscan deliciousness. For fancy meals, head to ambitious Oreade, helmed by culinary superwoman Giancarla Bodoni, whose team rigorously scours the local *campagna* for the very best produce and ingredients. Dishes change with the shifting moods of Mother Nature; previous highlights include smoked duck breast with micro-celery and green-apple sorbet, braised wild-boar short ribs, and chocolate fondant with liqueur-poached pears. Sit outside and your meal will come with a generous portion of Tuscan-tapestry views: all rippling hills, verdant valleys and painterly fields. The more casual (but just as lovely) *enoteca* entices with *bruschette*, tarts, salads, charcuterie and cheese plates. The library bar's terrace merits a bottle of prosecco or a bellini or three: it's ornamented with those stunning Val d'Orcia vistas, after all.

DRESS CODE

Linen, leather sandals, an unbuttoned shirt. A beatific expression and just-got-out-of-bed hair wouldn't go amiss, either.

'Sit outside and your meal will come with a generous portion of Tuscan-tapestry views: all rippling hills, verdant valleys and painterly fields.'

YUCATÁN MEXICO

Get a flavour of Mexico's colonial past at elegant Mérida, the vibrant capital of the Yucatán state, whose buildings blush prettily in pastel hues and whose neighbours include majestic Mayan ruins, soul-stirring cenotes and beatific beaches.

Shot in tropical temperatures between taco breaks

Coqui Coqui Mérida Residence & Spa

YUCATÁN, MEXICO

STYLE PERFUMED PIED-À-TERRE
SETTING MÉRIDA'S CENTRO HISTÓRICO

Power couples come in all shapes and sizes, but none are so lovely as Coqui Coqui Mérida's owners: Argentine model and perfumier Nicolas Malleville and his gorgeous Italian wife – and successful designer – Francesca Bonato. As Coqui Coqui, they've raised a thriving hotel family, with perfumed residences gracing locations across the Yucatán peninsula (Izamal, Coba, Valladolid, Mérida) and the South Pacific (Bora Bora). It's hard to pick a favourite from this bohemian tribe, but Mérida tugged at our heartstrings with particular gusto, on account of its solo suite. Nicolas and Francesca's love for Mexico – where they first met on a suitably sensational white-sand beach – shines through here. There's a perfumeria stocked with Coqui's own candles and fragrances; a boutique selling Coqui honey, *tisanas*, chocolates and treasure from home label Oficios Artesanos (clothing, homeware, travel essentials); plus a pretty courtyard café. It's stylish, relaxed and utterly seductive – just like its creators.

'We slip inside what looks like a closed shop
and climb the staircase to our dimly lit, romantically
scented quarters. We're a little bit margarita-buzzed
and it feels just a little bit special.'
STEPHANIE WATERMAN, STYLE SCOUT

THE FINER DETAILS

BEDTIME

L'Epicerie We're petitioning for more hotels with just one bedroom: what could be more romantic than having the whole place to yourselves? The rooftop L'Epicerie possesses more pizzazz than a whole wing of boudoirs bow-tied together. Decorated with Mexican tiles and berry-dark velvet curtains, the high-ceilinged suite also has a wrought-iron four-poster draped in white linen and thick, tasselled ropes. Dappled light filters through floor-to-ceiling glass doors, which open onto a balcony overlooking a tropical, plant-filled interior courtyard – which you'll share with approximately nobody. The elegant sitting room has two sofas and a café table; the Carrara marble-clad bathroom has a duo of majestic clawfoot tubs and a shower.

WORTH GETTING OUT OF BED FOR

Memory and scent are closely linked; ensure you never forget your stay here by picking up something from Coqui Coqui's perfumeria. (Kickstart your olfactory bulb – yes, that is the correct term – by wearing it here.) Yoga devotees can get their bendy fix by requesting a private session – with the option of pilates, too – in the comfort of the suite. Seeking some TLC? Opt for the sensuous spa's Coqui Coqui ritual, which features four different types of massage, a sugar-and-honey scrub, a detoxifying drink, a facial and a botanical bath to finish. Mérida, the Yucatán's cultured capital, has a rich artistic and architectural heritage; learn all about it on a walking tour. Marvel at pre-Columbian artefacts at the Museum of Anthropology and History (the Baroque-style building that houses it is equally impressive). Craving some beach time? Progresso's golden stretch of sand is a 25-minute drive from Mérida. If you want to learn more about perfume-making, Coqui Coqui's fragrant HQ is in Valladolid, a two-hour drive away.

FOOD AND DRINK

Pick your favourite table on the courtyard and settle in for a leisurely breakfast starring faultless coffee, buttery pastries and indulgent chocolates. Light lunches can be rustled up on request, but you'll need to head out for dinner (all the more reason to make the most of the enticing local restaurants). While you're here, go large on tacos, *tamales* (steamed doughy pockets stuffed with a variety of flavoursome fillings) and churros.

DRESS CODE

Be Coqui – wear whatever you want (you're the only guests, after all). Personally, we'd opt for silks, velvets, gemstones and a spritz of that signature scent.

'The rooftop L'Epicerie possesses more pizzazz than a whole wing of boudoirs bow-tied together.'

SAN FRANCISCO USA

Settled by seafaring Spaniards in the 18th century, populated by gold-digging dreamers in the 19th century, and rebuilt after a devastating earthquake the century after that, San Francisco has mastered the art of reinvention to become, well, the city of invention.

Captured on a clam chowder-worthy winter's day

The Battery

SAN FRANCISCO, USA

STYLE CLUB CLASSIC

SETTING BUZZING BAY AREA

Where does The Battery get its power from? A Midas-touch couple: Brit-hit entrepreneur Michael Birch and his tech-savvy American wife, Xochi. Their first collaboration: social-media giant Bebo. Their second? The Battery. (We can't wait for the third.) This buzzing magnet for San Fran creatives was conceived as a members' club, but bunking down in one of its boutique bedrooms gives guests access-all-areas privileges. Thanks to design maestro Ken Fulk, interiors are an inch-by-inch extravaganza of bold prints, caramel-coloured leather, charming curios, marble, glass and pops of colour. NB: Don't be fooled by the hotel's gadgety origins: here, guests are encouraged to recharge with a digital detox.

'Want a raucous night on the town?
Here you can indulge and still keep
your slippers on. Prefer to escape the
rabble? Your serene room will happily
oblige. This place is undeniably
one-of-a-kind.'

VICTORIA LEWIS, ON-THE-GO WRITER

THE FINER DETAILS

BEDTIME

The Penthouse If you wanted to form your own tech startup, there's room enough to establish your HQ in the palatial Penthouse, which sprawls across a whopping 575 m² (6,200 sq ft). Exposed steel beams, punchy masculine colours and a modern four-poster bed prove this suite means business. Admire your enormous private patio through the floor-to-ceiling windows, but do step outside – a barbecue, hot tub and panoramic city views await. (If you've befriended members of The Battery, invite them up, too – there's space for 14 around the outside dining table.) Stay buzzing with help from the in-suite espresso machine; when you want to take the pace down a notch or two, stake out the freestanding tub in the bathroom bathed in natural light. No doubt you'll be busy maximizing the hotel's excellent wining and dining options, but should you fancy a night 'in', the Penthouse has its own swish kitchen, equipped with top-of-the-line Viking appliances.

WORTH GETTING OUT OF BED FOR

Take time to appreciate your boutique basecamp's arty side by browsing its on-site exhibitions: featured artists have included Ana Teresa Fernández, Cortis & Sonderegger, Mira Dancy and William T. Wiley. Test out the gym (with state-of-the-art Cybex equipment) and spa, whose treatments include Swedish, deep-tissue, aromatherapy and hot-stone massages, and fire any dietary queries at the in-house nutritionist. This sociable members' club organizes an ever-changing roster of events to keep its people happy: community dinners, self-professed 'nerd nights', live-music specials, and more. Stellar drinking and dining options are only a short stroll away, as are prime waterfront views along the Embarcadero.

Hop on bikes and wheel through the Presidio, embark on a night tour of Alcatraz, or nab tickets to a San Francisco Giants game.

FOOD AND DRINK

Guests have a choice of places to clinch their deals (romantic or otherwise). There's the handsome House Bar, the brick-bedecked Living Room, the Musto Bar (where gentlemen are asked to behave as such; ladies, likewise), the sky-gazing Garden Bar and 717B restaurant, The Battery's beating heart (expect Cali-Med magic from the chef). The menu is split into 'Small' (manageable portions of seared foie gras with mandarin and pecan, or charred octopus with almond picada, for example) and 'Large' (try swordfish with fennel and horseradish, or lamb ragù with ricotta and pecorino). The Battery's Director of Wine, Christophe Tassan, is one of only 16 Meilleurs Ouvriers de France sommeliers in the world, so send any grape-related questions his way.

DRESS CODE

Less tech-geek, more tech-chic: Japanese denim; boxfresh Air Max; fashion-forward tailoring.

'Interiors are an inch-by-inch extravaganza of bold prints, caramel-coloured leather, charming curios, marble, glass and pops of colour.'

SUMBA INDONESIA

Seeking the next island paradise? Follow in the trail of the board-balancing surfers: they knew about Sumba before anyone else did. Twice the size of Bali, but with 15 per cent of its population, this underrated island is the real (Indonesian) thing.

Photographed after March's traditional jousting festival

Nihi Sumba

SUMBA, INDONESIA

STYLE HANG-TEN HEAVEN
SETTING INDONESIAN IDYLL

Once upon a time, a low-key beach hostel occupied Nihi Sumba's stretch of sand – boy, talk about an upgrade. Fashion mogul Chris Burch and hotelier-supremo James McBride clubbed together to re-imagine this paradisiacal plot of land, swapping the original frill-free sleeping quarters for 28 amped-up villas. They sealed the deal with the addition of a private beach with watersports facilities, a spa set in a sheltered creek framed by pandanus trees, an equestrian centre, a beach cinema and enough wining and dining options to satisfy the entire cast of *Point Break*. (Bring your board, by the way: this is surf central.)

'If you're after a true adventure "on the edge of wildness", but also want to be sure to have a cocktail in hand or a mind-bendingly luxurious massage at a moment's notice, get yourself to Nihi Sumba now.'

HENRIETTA THOMPSON, DESIGN AUTHORITY

THE FINER DETAILS

BEDTIME

Marrangga Wave Front One-Bedroom Villa
Isn't it time you slept al fresco on a cliffside *bale*, perched on a platform with jaw-dropping sea views? You can do exactly that at Marrangga (mosquito nets will ensure you slumber in unbitten peace). Of course, if you prefer to catch 40 winks inside, the king-size four-poster is pretty tempting, too. Acknowledging that nature really is rather special in these parts, Nihi Sumba's owners sensibly equipped the villa with a private garden, an outdoor shower and dining area, and a private plunge pool with a terrace. The conical roof, thatched with *alang-alang* grass, honours traditional design; added local flavour comes courtesy of Sumbanese antiques, island wood and ikat prints.

WORTH GETTING OUT OF BED FOR

Take one of the hotel's sweet-natured steeds out for a ride: canter along the beach or trot through the bush. (You could also hire motorbikes and zip around the island.) Dip into the astonishingly aquamarine waters of the Weekuri lagoon. Visit a local village and watch ikat fabrics being made, or admire the majestic stone tombstones that are dotted about the island. Keen surfers can acquaint themselves with the world-famous break, nicknamed 'Occy's Left' in honour of champion surfer Mark Occhilupo (or just referred to reverently as 'the wave'). Perfect your *vinyasas* with a private or group yoga class at the hotel. Journey to a secluded valley (and its quartet of bamboo-bedecked couples' treatment rooms) for the NihiOka Spa Safari: choose a homemade aromatic oil and indulge in a stress-busting massage with views of peaceful paddy fields.

FOOD AND DRINK

Nihi Sumba's rates include all your food and (non-alcoholic) drink, so make the most of both. (This isn't difficult, since the bars rustle up fruit-infused daiquiris, rum-addled caipirinhas and an excellent mojito made with home-grown mint, and the restaurants champion the region's seafood fantasia.) Nibble sashimi with sundowners or swing by the Boat House bar for one of its magic barbecues. Flit to the Nest, perched in a treehouse platform above a rugged stretch of coast, for a lunch you'll remember for all the right reasons. You can also request a lip-smacking lobster feast in the privacy of your own wave-lapped villa, or have a grilled-meat feast on a torch-lit beach.

DRESS CODE

Off-duty surfer with a hot dinner date: model tropical prints, shell jewelry and salt-sprayed locks.

'Isn't it time you slept al fresco on a cliffside *bale*, perched on a platform with jaw-dropping sea views?'

COTSWOLDS UK

England's green and pleasant credentials crescendo at
this designated Area of Outstanding Natural Beauty,
immortalized by Laurie Lee and endorsed by royalty. The
five characterful counties – Wiltshire, Gloucestershire,
Oxfordshire, Warwickshire and Worcestershire – are home
to charming hamlets, snuggly inns and delicious dairy highs.

Captured in the first blushes of autumn

Foxhill Manor

COTSWOLDS, UK

STYLE TO THE MANOR BORN
SETTING SWEET VALLEY HIGH

Rock 'n' roll isn't usually synonymous with Cotswolds country living – but it turns out a fair few platinum-record artists share a crush on this honey-hued hideaway with A-list credentials. No doubt the big-name fans went gaga (or should that be Gaga?) for this private-house hotel's relaxed philosophy and just-as-you-like service. Eschewing the usual formalities (check-in, for example), Foxhill Manor invites you to treat every bit of it as your own: help yourself to drinks, plan your menu with the chef, and be as idle or as active as you like. Generous daily supplies of on-the-house shortbread and just-baked cake enhance the home-from-home feel. All in all, Foxhill is as deliciously refreshing as its signature G&Ts.

'If you want to pretend you're Anna Wintour and madly request lobsters at 3am and snow in July, the staff here would rise to the challenge. They truly want you to be happy, relaxed and have a good time.'

OLIVIA VON HALLE, PYJAMA QUEEN

THE FINER DETAILS

BEDTIME

Oak Suite A modern wooden four-poster and caramel-coloured, wood-clad floors earn this devilishly romantic suite its name. Two clawfoot tubs by the mullioned windows and an autumnal lounge area (home to the manor's original fireplace) are your additional cues to snuggle up. There are cosy, cushioned window nooks galore, a pair of Bruno Mathsson-designed 'Jetson' recliners and a dining table with space for four – the white fur rugs add a dash of Scandi sex appeal. Gadget junkies, you'll have a TV, tablet computer, Ruark digital radio and a Nespresso machine to fiddle with – make ours a macchiato.

WORTH GETTING OUT OF BED FOR

Pretend you're landed gentry and set off to explore the estate in wellies and tweed; you could also gad about on a bike or atop a trusty steed. Foxhill's big sister (and near neighbour Dormy House) has a star-turn spa and guests here get free access to its impressive facilities – obliging hotel staff will whisk you there and back. Forget the local Odeon: Foxhill Manor has its own screening room with Fatboy bean bags, an enviable stash of DVDs and on-the-house popcorn. Lovebirds: request the key to the estate's secret Japanese Garden and get amorous in leafy, secluded splendour.

FOOD AND DRINK

Foxhill prides itself on doing things differently: although its restaurant has a menu, guests are encouraged to sit down for a tasty tête-à-tête with the hotel's Michelin-starred chef at the beginning of their stay to personalize their dining experience. Impromptu barbecues and picnics can be arranged; with a bit more notice, Foxhill can even rustle up a spit-roasted ox (channel your inner Henry VIII). The Dining Room bar has a stout stash of wines, ales, ciders and spirits; enjoy them in the convivial Living Room or out on the terrace.

DRESS CODE

Come with Barbour, ardour and bling.

'Request the key to the estate's secret Japanese Garden and get amorous in leafy, secluded splendour.'

MARRAKECH
MOROCCO

Founded by the Almoravids around 1062
and backdropped by the Atlas mountains,
Marrakech's charms include the UNESCO-
listed Medina, Berber influences, sociable *souks*
and labyrinthine streets, where light-dappled
courtyards hide behind heavy studded doors.

Shot on a winter evening between calls to prayer

Riad de Tarabel

MARRAKECH, MOROCCO

STYLE MELLOW MOORISH MANSION
SETTING SECRET MEDINA SIDESTREET

Dodging donkeys, mopeds and haggling *souk* stall-owners in the tangled streets of Marrakech's Medina can feel a lot like existing in a high-speed video game. Slow things down at Riad de Tarabel: a hushed, hidden kingdom of orange trees, orientalist murals and quiet courtyards, decorated with flocks of stuffed birds in ornamental cages, vintage peacock chairs and cloud-white roses. Rooms are perfumed with jasmine, rosewater and tuberose, and enlivened with antiques and curios handpicked by the elegant French owner, Rose Marie. Helpful staff dressed in low-slung, white-linen trousers, Converse sneakers and red Fez hats are your discreet attendants at this grey-and-honey *riad*, which impresses by day and wows with candlelight by night. Guests can pretend that they have the whole place to themselves – bedroom doors don't even have locks, adding to the private-home feel. Chirruping birds, trickling water fountains and the rhythmic calls to prayer are your soundtrack here.

'It's luxurious enough to make you feel spoilt, without making you worry about spilling your sun cream. It feels like a home away from home, albeit nicer than our actual home – and with staff.'

KATIE TREGGIDEN, DESIGN JOURNALIST

THE FINER DETAILS

BEDTIME

Junior Suite You'll be retiling your bedroom back home, mentally at least, after a stay in Riad de Tarabel's Junior Suite, bedecked with beautiful patterned Moroccan tiles (designed by the owner herself) and antique French furniture. Canoodle on the cosy daybed by the window, or admire the courtyard and its water feature from the comfort of your bed. The suite has a clawfoot tub in the bedroom, designed for sociable sudsing sessions, plus a rain-head shower; maximize those amber-scented Ortigia unguents. You'll be treated to house-made pastries and mint tea each afternoon; guests are also given an on-loan mobile phone and map of Marrakech.

WORTH GETTING OUT OF BED FOR

The concierge can arrange treks and tours: hop in a 4×4 and head to Berber villages, the Plateau de Kik, Ourika Valley or Lake Takerkoust. Hot-air balloon adventures and camel- or horse-riding treks to the desert or mountains can also be arranged. Practise your haggling skills at the sensuous *souks*; by night, try pigeon pie, potato-and-egg sandwiches, harissa soup and other local delicacies from the stalls at the Djemaa el-Fnaa. (Admire the snake charmers, belly-dancers and *gnawa* musicians, too.) Lovers have been making a beeline for Le Jardin Majorelle since the gorgeous gardens first opened to the public in 1947; follow in their footsteps. Back 'home', cool off in the adults-only, black-granite pool and watch the sun set over the Medina rooftops from the roof-terrace cabana. Staff will bring up drinks, lanterns and blankets, so you can stay put for a spot of stargazing.

FOOD AND DRINK

In keeping with its deliciously relaxed feel, Riad de Tarabel is a menu-free zone; just let staff know if you're hungry and they'll suggest something delicious. Traditional Moroccan dishes (try the egg-and-meatball tagine) are available for lunch and dinner; dine *à deux* whenever and wherever you like. Breakfast is definitely worth getting out of bed for: head to the rooftop terrace or one of the cosy salon areas for moreish Moroccan crêpes, pâtisserie, homemade yogurt, apricot jam, fresh orange juice, mint tea and coffee.

DRESS CODE

Tap into Marrakech's hippie history and unleash your inner beatnik: model ethereal frocks, rough linens, hammered-silver jewelry, loose-collared shirts in vibrant hues – and a dash of pomegranate or rose scent. Mrs Smiths could pick up a garnet- or citrine-coloured wrap from the on-site boutique.

'Cool off in the adults-only, black-granite pool and watch the sun set over the Medina rooftops from the roof-terrace cabana.'

NEW YORK USA

If ever a metropolis needed no introduction, it's this one –
eternal muse to countless poets and writers, directors and
starlets, rappers and singers. Bring your energetic side for the
Big Apple's big-name draws, A+ eateries, dive bars, flea markets
and urban thrills. With all this on its plate (and more), it's no
wonder New York is the city that never sleeps.

Snapped as Brooklyn glowed in spring

The Williamsburg Hotel

NEW YORK, USA

STYLE BRICKING IT

SETTING HIPSTER HEARTLAND

The Williamsburg Hotel, standing like an on-trend totem on Wythe Avenue, has more than its fair share of street cred. Designed by London-based starchitects Michaelis Boyd (Babington House, the Groucho Club, Soho House Berlin), this hotel is Brooklyn-baby to the core. Industrial-chic interiors riff on the area's gritty working-class past, with pops of colour, bespoke furnishings by Bill Amberg Studio and the handsome Harvey restaurant adding comfort to the cool. Instead of uniforms, staff sport their favourite threads; rooms are kitted out with nifty MediaHub technology and breakfast is served pretty much all day (there's even a hipster take on high tea). A ravishing rooftop pool, unique water-tower bar and striking ballroom are the icing on this Big Apple. NB: Dog-lovers, rejoice – Fido can come, too.

'There's a lot to make eyes at inside this room. Can a wooden floor be sexy? I'd argue yes – and have 21 pictures of the beautifully constructed chevron-patterned boards to prove it.'

GEMMA ASKHAM, ROAMING WRITER

THE FINER DETAILS

BEDTIME

Skyline Suite For views to rival Brooklyn's bird's nests, opt for the Skyline Suite, whose chief charm is its impressive private terrace with unobstructed Manhattan-skyline vistas. Additional enticements include a stylish separate seating area, oak floors, floor-to-ceiling windows and bespoke furnishings. The marble and brass-accented bathroom (embellished with Waterworks fittings) has a tempting bathtub; unleash the locally loved Apotheke bath products while you soak. Indulge your inner geek via the in-room MediaHub Mini, which lets you stream music and project videos from your mobile device. Then there's that tempting king-size bed – and you've got twin showers to undress for, too.

WORTH GETTING OUT OF BED FOR

Unwind in the pretty front terrace, just below street level, which is covered in greenery and decorated with artworks by local creatives. For a Brooklyn-via-Bangkok experience, head out in one of the hotel's tuk-tuks and explore the area's boutiques, galleries, bars and restaurants. Come summer, hit that sceney, scenic rooftop pool. By night, listen to live music – local jazz cats, perhaps – in the lobby. Go bowling at Brooklyn Bowl or the Gutter Bar; sip craft brews at Brooklyn Brewery; hunt for local treasure at Brooklyn Flea. The hotel can sign you up for a range of tours: admire street art in Bushwick, tick off some of the best bars and restaurants with help from a clued-up local, discover the Jewish quarter, go on a literary tour, and more. Last, but definitely not least, nip to Manhattan by water taxi or stroll across the iconic bridge.

FOOD AND DRINK

Breakfast is a pleasingly long affair, available from 7am until 4pm. Start the day, Brooklyn-style, by opting for the hash-brown sandwich. Locality shapes Harvey's menu: bread and pastries are sourced from Brooklyn Bread Lab; the moreish pizzas are made with freshly milled Bushwick flour; seasonal 'Garden' dishes showcase meat and produce from neighbourhood suppliers. (We'd order the spicy fried pumpkin and miso Brussels sprouts again in a heartbeat.) For libations, there's the Instagram-worthy water-tower bar; the lobby bar is decorated with a rainbow-hued installation by local street artist Eric Reiger. Exposed brick, a hardwood parquet floor, mood lighting, turquoise barber-style leather stools and dashes of colour and velvet continue the factory-fabulous feel; the bar itself is made up of artfully arranged wooden picture frames.

DRESS CODE

Born in Brooklyn. Start with deliberately dishevelled denim and bookish specs. Kudos for sporting sustainable fashion by local, eco-smart brands such as Kaight and Coclico.

'A ravishing rooftop pool, unique water-tower bar and striking ballroom are the icing on this Big Apple.'

PATAGONIA CHILE

Follow in the sizable footsteps of mythical Chilean giants –
mentioned in medieval postcards written by Portuguese explorers
– to Patagonia, stomping ground of the 'Bigfeet'. Very, very tall
locals aside, this vast region divided by the Andes mountains
is a rugged fusion of fjords and forests.

Photographed under the sulky skies of spring

Awasi Patagonia

TORRES DEL PAINE, CHILE

STYLE CALL OF THE WILD

SETTING NO COUNTRY FOR OLD MEN

The Torres del Paine national park in the foothills of Patagonia ('Land of the Bigfeet') is home to Awasi. It's also home to the guanaco, a thick-skinned (literally) camelid native to South America. (Guanaco fact: one male has up to 100 female concubines, who he guards with savage pride.) Should you wish to bring 100 lovers with you to Awasi, you'd have more than enough room: each of the hotel's 14 luxury lodges occupies its own secluded pocket of this rugged 11,000-acre reserve. Your neighbours? Foxes, eagles, horses, sheep, gauchos, and perhaps a roaming puma or two. Forget dog-eared pamphlets on the local area: guests here get their own private guide-cum-driver, so you can conquer the wilderness on your doorstep. Post-adventure, a malbec-heavy wine cellar, relaxed restaurant and hot tub-toting decks await.

'The bathtub beckons; pressed up against
the window and awash with fragrant froth.
As I settle in and stretch out, the sky begins
to blush, bestowing a celestial glow upon the
peaks beneath. It's pure sorcery.'

HARRIET CHARNOCK-BATES, HOTEL-HOPPING EDITOR

THE FINER DETAILS

BEDTIME

The Master Villa Pretend you're the sole pioneers on the frontier in the Master Villa, the most secluded of the hotel's sleeping quarters (trust us, that's saying something). The design of the 14 villas is based loosely on the traditional gaucho outposts that were once dotted about the *estancia*. We say 'loosely', because now they come with a king-size bed, a cosy living area with a fireplace, an iPod dock, minibar, Nespresso machine and L'Occitane bath products. To help you snuggle up in style, each villa is kitted out with cosy sheepskin rugs, wool blankets and wood-burning stoves. One reproach you won't be able to level at Awasi Patagonia is a dearth of windows: the romantically remote villas feature multiple viewing points of that staggering scenery. After an adventurous day of exploring, dunk yourself in your al fresco hot tub – head or legs first, as you see fit.

WORTH GETTING OUT OF BED FOR

'Torres del Paine' may sound like the name of a terrifying Chilean wrestler, but don't be scared, it's very lovely – and very worth exploring. Go on a guided trek to the base of the park's namesake three granite towers; you could also conquer the scenery atop a horse or from the comfort of a 4WD. When night falls, set off on a twinkly stargazing expedition; alternatively, stay 'in' and count the constellations from the comfort of your hot tub. Suffering some post-galloping rump-ache? Request an in-room couple's massage ...

FOOD AND DRINK

This is no time to get sentimental about the guanaco you may or may not have befriended during your adventures, since Awasi dishes them up in its restaurant. Carnivores can sample them in tartare or steak form (best paired with a punchy malbec). Seafood also gets a look in; the local hake is a highlight. Guac-addicts will love the breakfast spreads, which include cheese, meats and mounds of the green stuff; there's also a DIY juice bar (whip up your favourite energizing blend) and hot options. A bovine-chic bar area awaits in the main lodge; let the resident mixologist cater to your tastes, or sip a Chilean red. You won't want to stray any further for food and drink – the hotel's rates include all your meals and tipples. Besides, round here, the nearest eatery is a 10-hour trek away.

DRESS CODE

Get your gaucho fantasies well and truly out of your system by modelling alpaca wool, leather and earthy hues of russet, ochre and gold. *Bombacha* trousers and straw *chupalla* hats might be over-egging the custard, mind ...

'Your neighbours? Foxes, eagles, horses, sheep, gauchos, and perhaps a roaming puma or two.'

MEDHUFARU
MALDIVES

This pearl of the Indian Ocean has been lavished with more 'island paradise', 'tropical treat' and 'azure waters' clichés than its beaches have grains of sand. Luckily, the island lives up to every one of them – and its wildlife-rich patches of jungle and vibrant culture deserve special mention, too.

Photographed while lobsters lolled offshore

Soneva Jani

MEDHUFARU, MALDIVES

STYLE OVERWATER WORLD
SETTING ISLAND QUINTET

Rules and romance don't usually go together – unless you're at Soneva Jani, which operates a strict 'no news, no shoes' policy. (We endorse this, since neither belong in the bedroom.) Besides its eye-popping location in the aquamarine Noonu Atoll, the hotel has a quite frankly ridiculous list of lures. There's an observatory, a cinema, a watersports and dive centre, a spa and deliciously chilled chocolate, cheese and ice-cream rooms – all perched above the glittering ocean like majestic resting turtles. This eco-conscious aquatic playground sprawls spectacularly across five castaway islands and a tranquil lagoon; bonus points for the hotel's Mr and Ms Friday butlers (inspired by Robinson Crusoe's island companion).

'By the time we discovered our villa, I actually
contemplated forgoing sleep. Why would any sane
person miss a single moment in this place?'

IROSHINI CHUA, JET-SET DOCTOR

THE FINER DETAILS

BEDTIME

One-Bedroom Water Retreat with Slide
Soneva's vast Water Retreat somehow manages to satisfy heart-fluttering honeymoon hankerings and big-kid dreams with its full-size pool, terrace, retractable roof (which you can operate while lying in bed: stargaze while you starfish) and, yes, a giant water slide to whoosh you from the deck straight into the waves. As tempting as it might be to spend your entire stay in or under water, do at least *try* to make it back to dry land; you wouldn't want to miss out on those walk-in minibars (with wine and Nespresso machines) or that butler service, after all. Modest types: bring swimwear that can withstand the gravitational pull of that water slide.

WORTH GETTING OUT OF BED FOR

Having admired each other, appraise the reef with help from the resident marine biologist. Look for sea turtles and manta rays in the Noonu Atoll, or unlock the secrets of the local dive sites alongside multilingual PADI instructors. Go kayaking, paddleboarding, surfing, windsurfing and kitesurfing, or join a catamaran safari to spot gambolling dolphins. Banish your body's blues at the lagoon-spying spa, surrounded by turquoise waters; the coconut scrub includes a liberal application of its namesake oil – your skin will feel softer than a buttered lobster's. Sail to Soneva Jani's equally enticing sister, Soneva Fushi, in the hotel's yacht (the trip takes half a day; nip there in a speedboat if you can't wait that long). We can't think of many hotels that come with a resident astronomer, so make the most of this one; you could join an astronomical dinner cruise, have a midnight star-spotting picnic or get up early for sunrise astronomy.

FOOD AND DRINK

Meals are served at the Gathering, an open-air pontoon perch armed with water slides and #nofilter views galore. Get your five dailies at So Fresh, which earns its name with vitamin-packed juices, salads and mains, or opt for experimental wine tastings and grape-matched dinners at So Imaginative. Temperature rising? Head to So Cool for on-the-house helpings of ice cream, chocolate and cheese; you can also stockpile sushi, sashimi and wine to take back to your oceanic sleeping quarters. For tropical smoothies, cocktails or a flute of frosty fizz, hit the Gathering Bar. Have an out-of-this-world meal at the observatory, where a quartet of tables can be set up, each one linked to screens connected to the hotel's telescope. You could also hop in a boat to Zuhair's Island for a private lunch or dinner, or try So Engaging: a five-course, chef's-table mystery menu.

DRESS CODE

Pearl-white layers; splashes of blue/Chanel Bleu; a shell or two.

'Modest types: bring swimwear that can withstand the gravitational pull of that water slide.'

TORRES VEDRAS
PORTUGAL

This seaside city knows a thing or two about acting defensive: its
redoubtable 19th-century fortresses – the 'Lines of Torres Vedras'
– put it on the map, after all. These days, the Blue Flag beaches
and rolling emerald hills are a much more peaceful proposition.

Captured just before a biblical storm swept by

Areias do Seixo

TORRES VEDRAS, PORTUGAL

STYLE EARTH, WIND AND FIRE
SETTING RUGGED COSTA DE PRATA

We're not in the habit of writing Portuguese fairy tales, but if we were, we'd set them in Torres Vedras: a wild, sea salt-sprayed patch of the Atlantic Coast, home to the equally wild – and whimsical – Areias do Seixo. Don't be deceived by the futuristic glass-and-steel architecture: this big-hearted hotel puts nature first. Exhibit one: the restaurant, where just-plucked vegetables from the greenhouse and garden take centre stage. Exhibit two: the chalk-and-blackboard activities list, which encourages guests to get out into that majestic scenery (mussels-foraging *à deux*, perhaps?) From mussels to muscles: unknot and unwind yours in the spoiling spa, or stretch them out by your bohemian bedside fireplace. This hotel is a certified firestarter – head to its twice-weekly bonfire if you don't believe us.

'After years of thinking about it, I know exactly what comprises a good building: it's one that makes you feel engaged, optimistic, pleased, flattered. Areias do Seixo does all of that.'

STEPHEN BAYLEY, CULTURE CONNOISSEUR

THE FINER DETAILS

BEDTIME

Love Room Nha Cretcheu The name says it all – it's practically illegal *not* to get romantic in any of Areias do Seixo's four Love Rooms. Possibly the fairest of them all, Nha Cretcheu has an elevated four-poster bed with a frame hewn from wooden boughs, plus a fireplace by the bed with a stash of logs, so you can stoke the flames. (Flammable nightwear: best left at home.) Chandelier lights with spaghetti-thin crystalline threads add glitter; pulse-quickening extras include the Jacuzzi tub, outdoor shower and garden-spying behemoth of a bathtub.

WORTH GETTING OUT OF BED FOR

Get green-fingered in the garden and pick the juiciest specimens for dinner, or stroll across the protected dunes and collect fresh mussels from the beach (the hotel's chefs will help you cook your loot). Guests with an eco-conscience can take part in 'feel green' activities: an agricultural lesson with a local farmer, perhaps. Reward your labours in the sanctuary of the spa, where a sauna, Turkish bath, two massage rooms and a relaxation room await. There are no TVs in the bedrooms, but couch potatoes can get their digital fix with a trip to the 7th Art Room, which has a big screen, around 90 titles and tempting home-baked snacks. Take the boat across to Berlenga Grande island or learn to surf at the closest beach, Praia do Seixo. Back at boutique basecamp, sociable Areias hosts regular bonfires with on-the-house nibbles, wine and traditional Portuguese folk music. This hotel has a soft spot for events-planning: enjoy a private dinner in the pine forest, followed by your own film-screening; dine by the lake, or in a bedroom glimmering with candles; or take a chef-prepped picnic to the beach.

FOOD AND DRINK

Familiarize yourself with Portugal's bountiful larder (seafood is a highlight) at the romantic, relaxed restaurant, where a natural-mystic mood meets modish sophistication, courtesy of a sparkling chandelier and mismatched colourful chairs. Iberian pork and market-fresh fish are cooked to perfection on the wood oven and charcoal grill; go large when it comes to vegetables. You'll also want to try the hotel's homemade lemongrass tea and just-baked bread and cakes. Distinguished from the dining room by some artfully placed furniture, the bar is suited to conversations and rum-splashed, herb-bedecked cocktails. Panoramic windows open out to a sleek terrace, the gardens and the sea beyond; snuggle up by the fire pit with a warming glass of port. Still thirsty? Head to one of the local vineyards: Adega Mãe is our favourite.

DRESS CODE

High-class hippie: putty- and pewter-hued linen layers for floating around in; hammered-metal jewelry and a dash of sea-scented cologne.

'The name says it all – it's practically illegal not to get romantic in any of Areias do Seixo's Love Rooms.'

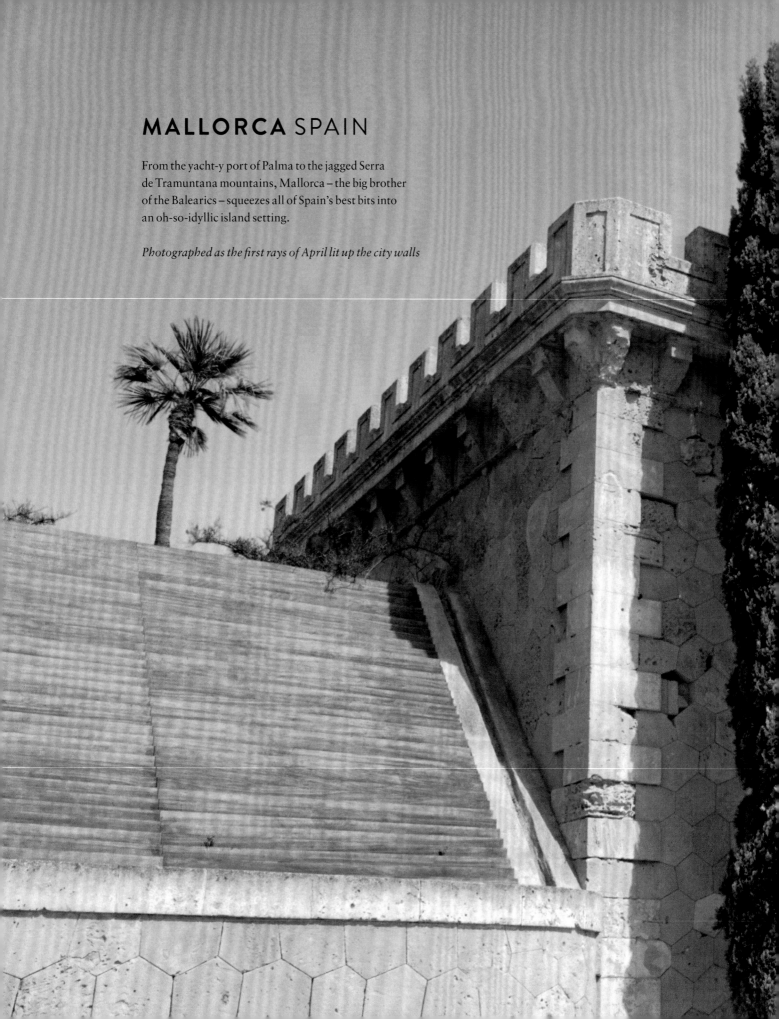

MALLORCA SPAIN

From the yacht-y port of Palma to the jagged Serra
de Tramuntana mountains, Mallorca – the big brother
of the Balearics – squeezes all of Spain's best bits into
an oh-so-idyllic island setting.

Photographed as the first rays of April lit up the city walls

Cap Rocat

MALLORCA, SPAIN

STYLE CLIFF-CLINGING FORTRESS
SETTING PALMA'S LIFE AQUATIC

Make love not war at Cap Rocat, a former military fortress hidden on a cliff in a peaceful pocket of the Bay of Palma. More heritage site than hotel, its defensive paraphernalia – a drawbridge, bunkers and trenches – provide a dramatic setting for pared-down boutique bedrooms, a dazzling infinity pool and two tempting restaurants. There is also a private, 2-km (1.2-mile) stretch of glittering coastline at your disposal. Spanish architect Antonio Obrador masterminded the transformation, turning shooting pads into sleeping quarters and re-imagining the original kitchen as an atmospheric setting for wine tastings and private dining. Need further proof that Cap Rocat comes in peace? Eco-concerns are taken seriously here: food is sourced from local farms; the al fresco saltwater pool is chlorine-free; recycling is a priority; and the hotel's flora is precision-planted to require minimal watering. We surrender.

'As I gaze over the Bay of Palma, I spy a local man enjoying his dip au naturel. Even an exposed bottom cannot interrupt the calm sophistication that pervades this beautifully thought-through hotel, perched on the cliff.'

JULES MCKEEN, ADLAND SUPERMUM

THE FINER DETAILS

BEDTIME

Sentinels Hidden away in the cliffs, all but invisible from the sea, the Sentinels' three rooms were originally the fort's lookout stations over the Bay of Palma. These historic hideaways still have their rough rock walls, but wooden finishes, mirrors and Mediterranean fabrics soften the effect. Their not-so-secret weapon is the eye-widening terrace, home to a sparkling infinity plunge pool overlooking the bay; you can continue to soak up the aquatic views from your king-size bed. Wash off the sand from the day's adventures in the romantic bathroom's generous tub and shower, making the most of those aromatic, locally made bath products.

WORTH GETTING OUT OF BED FOR

The hotel provides snorkelling equipment, so that guests can explore the marine reserve. There's a stash of on-loan mountain bikes, and the charming staff will point you towards suggested routes. Borrow rackets and balls and test out the clay tennis courts. The fortress's former kitchen is used for private dining and cookery classes: whip up a three-course meal with help from the chef, then sit down and enjoy it. Cap Rocat also has a list of individually priced activities and experiences, including sailing, deep-sea fishing, diving, horse-riding, pilates, yoga, helicopter or boat charters, and guided visits to local street markets and cultural hotspots. Palma is a 15-minute drive away: browse its local boutiques for beachwear, have a wave-side lunch and finish off with cocktails in a glitzy bar.

FOOD AND DRINK

Enjoy decadent wine-matched dinners at La Fortaleza, set in one of the main pavilions. The Mallorquin cuisine tips its sailor cap to the ocean: standout dishes include scorpion-fish *suquet* (seafood-and-potato stew), mussels, and curried mackerel with almonds. Sit out on the roof under the shade, looking out to sea. During the warm and balmy summer months, eat at the Sea Club, an open-air restaurant by the waterfront in the Queen's Cove. The relaxed culinary offerings include refreshing salads, flavoursome pasta dishes and grilled meats and seafood. NB: Order breakfast to your room: a generous spread of fresh fruit, homemade pastries, yogurt and jam will materialize at your door in a picnic hamper, and be set up for you to enjoy at your table.

DRESS CODE

Holidaying militia or washed-up mermaid/ merman: nautical stripes and gold frogging, or blue and coral accents, plus natural pearls for the Mrs.

'The suite's not-so-secret weapon is the eye-widening terrace, home to a sparkling infinity plunge pool overlooking the bay.'

GRINDAVIK ICELAND

Your local swimming pool will never look the same after a trip to this former fishing village, which shot to prominence with the creation of the Blue Lagoon: an astonishingly blue geothermal spa, surrounded by an otherworldly centuries-old lava field.

Photographed as the spring mists crept cloudily above the waters

The Retreat at Blue Lagoon

GRINDAVIK, ICELAND

STYLE OTHERWORLDLY SPA STAR
SETTING EXPLORER'S WET DREAM

Baby, it's cold outside. (This is the UNESCO-listed Reykjanes Geopark, where the Mid-Atlantic Ridge comes ashore, after all.) The only sensible response to such surroundings is to warm up, sharpish, in misty geothermal waters, a subterranean spa and Scandi-dandy rooms. Luckily, you can do all that and more at this ravishing Retreat, which lords it over a private patch of Iceland's world-famous Blue Lagoon. Not content with merely straddling this beautiful landscape, the hotel's rule-breakers went underground, too, carving out a maestro spa from a lava flow. The suites' private lagoons were formed by blowing up volcanic rock, then filling the holes with water; each of the pools is a different shape and size, depending on the vim and vigour of its explosion. Land of fire and ice, indeed.

'The Retreat exemplifies the Blue Lagoon's beautiful contradictions, as the heat from 800-year-old lava flow meets impeccable chill in its labyrinthine underground spa, and with the steaming cyan views outside every window.'

LAURA SNAPES, CULTURED CRITIC

THE FINER DETAILS

BEDTIME

The Lagoon Suite Pretend you're sleeping inside an enormous ice cube in this glittering suite, with floor-to-ceiling windows that let the (mind-bending) outdoors in. (Nobody can spy on *you*, though, since the suites are surrounded by privacy-providing lava.) Less well-endowed rooms have a private plunge pool; the Lagoon Suite has an astonishingly aqua, mineral-rich lagoon. Reverse the cruel hand of time by immersing yourself in its (allegedly) beauty-boosting waters. Bed down here and you'll be treated to a holiday's worth of on-the-house extras, including Blue Lagoon skin products, Icelandic beer and soft drinks, daily guided group hikes and yoga, copious servings of coffee in the lounge, access to a charming host and concierge, and use of the fitness centre.

WORTH GETTING OUT OF BED FOR

First things first: the Blue Lagoon, where Icelanders disrobe companionably for bathtime. Encircled by water, the hotel has its own private lagoon, accessed via the spa – so, unlike everyone else, you won't have to share. 'Spa' doesn't quite sum up the Retreat's geothermal wonderland of labyrinthine sanctuaries: opt for a massage, unwind on the panoramic viewing deck and count your goosebumps at the cold air well, before steaming things up again in the lagoon. After breakfast in the spa's restaurant, opt for the mineral package and be pampered with salts, silica and natural algae treatments. Landlubbers can join a guided hike to the Mid-Atlantic Ridge or head to Reykjavik, the island's small-but-mighty capital, a 40-minute drive away, where a charming old town and stellar restaurants await. Skidoo safaris and tours can be arranged; swap the metaphorical wild goose for the elusive Northern Lights in season.

FOOD AND DRINK

Meals at Moss restaurant come with a generous side of geology, thanks to gorgeous views of the local waters and their craggy outcrops; a stark metal-and-white dining room mirrors the sci fi-worthy setting. Get a flavour of Iceland's farms, fjords, mountains and waters thanks to the menu, which flexes with the seasons and shines a spotlight on local producers and ingredients. Book the chef's table and opt for the five- or seven-course tasting menu; the just-caught fish is a highlight. Continue your love-in with the local landscape at the Lounge, which serves irreproachable cocktails and hors d'oeuvres worth writing home about. Don't miss a wine-tasting session in the hotel's atmospheric underground cellar – you almost have to abseil into it.

DRESS CODE

Imagine Ranulph Fiennes or Ernie Shackleton on a blind date. White and silver, snuggly knitwear, leather accents and icicle-sparkle. If you're struggling, fashion-forward Scandi designers such as Astrid Andersen and Nicholas Nybro will come to your rescue.

'Less well-endowed hotel rooms have a private plunge pool; this has a steam-shrouded, astonishingly aqua, mineral-rich lagoon.'

HONG KONG CHINA

Adventures – culinary or otherwise – come in every flavour in Hong Kong, which delivers a heady taste of the Chinese high life. The skyscraper-studded horizon, mega-malls and island draws are immediately obvious; uncovering Hong Kong's wildlife, its secret bars and shophouse food-gems require more thorough exploration.

Captured on a close February morning

The Upper House

HONG KONG, CHINA

STYLE HEIGHT OF LUXURY
SETTING ARTERIAL ADMIRALTY

As debuts go, the Upper House takes some beating. It's hard to believe that this art-stuffed, sky-tickling triumph was the very first hotel project from homegrown hero André Fu (who would go for gold again with Smith-approved follow-ups Villa la Coste in Provence and the Fullerton Bay Hotel in Singapore). Many of Fu's signature flourishes were planted as sartorial seedlings here: a playful way with proportion; an abundance of natural materials; and a soothing sense of relaxed luxury (plus plenty of thoughtful extras: in-room yoga mats, slippers, an on-the-house 'maxi' bar). Food, wine and service are pretty much faultless (including a best-in-class concierge), and you'll have better views than the feathered locals: the Upper House nests in the heights of a 49-storey building in the Pacific Place complex.

'I succumb to a bubble bath. As I survey the
nightscape, Mr Smith alerts me to a note:
"Please remember the view may be a two-
way one" – but I love the thought of high-rise
voyeurism between consenting skyscrapers.'

IMMODESTY BLAIZE, PROFESSIONAL BOMBSHELL

THE FINER DETAILS

BEDTIME

Studio 70 Harbour View Forget Studio 54, we're into Studio 70. The Upper House's bedrooms start on the 38th floor; this particular lofty perch equates to front-row views of Victoria Harbour and the emerald hills beyond from the bamboo-bedecked bedroom. The beckoning bed, modern art, striking sculptures and cultured tomes provide additional eye candy; for actual candy, raid the maxi-bar's jars of chocolates, cookies and apple crisps. We'd happily camp out in the spectacular bathroom, whose centrepiece is a giant limestone-clad tub. Sudsing here has an added frisson (and we're not just talking about the bounty of botanical Bamford bath products): thanks to all that mirrored glass, you can see the whole of Hong Kong while you're naked – and vice versa.

WORTH GETTING OUT OF BED FOR

Take your cue from those views: stroll to the harbour and explore the lively Kowloon district (known as Hong Kong's 'dark side'), pausing in the bars, boutiques and restaurants. Below you, the monolithic Pacific Place mall awaits, home to a wallet-emptying array of upscale designer shops and a whole holiday's worth of dining and drinking options. Stroll the leafy lengths of Bowen Road, or try free yoga on the lawn on weekend mornings. Admire the Upper House's extensive art collection: you'll have already seen British designer Thomas Heatherwick's clever exterior cladding at street level on arrival; head higher up to see *Rise*, a 10-storey, water-inspired installation by Hiroshiwata Sawada. Tropical Hong Kong Park – a serene green expanse, perfect for walking, jogging or watching locals perform tai chi – is just five minutes' walk from the hotel. From the park, it's a short stroll to the Garden Road terminus, where you can buy tickets for the famous tram up to Victoria Peak with its jaw-dropping views, both en route and at the summit.

FOOD AND DRINK

In a city famed for culinary highlights, Café Gray Deluxe strikes a high note – and not just because it's on the ear-popping 49th floor. Expect star-turn comfort food from global-superstar chef Gray Kunz: dishes such as shrimp-and-pork dumplings with black-mushroom broth, or the signature steak tartare *ketjap*. Stunning views, flawless cocktails at the long bar, and Fu star-styling keep the discerning locals coming back for more. Book one of the snug private dining pods by the open kitchen and order after-dinner coffee, if only for their accompaniment: generous slabs of broken chocolate that make After Eights pale in comparison, or swing by during the day for the equally brilliant afternoon tea.

DRESS CODE

Your birthday suit for the view-tiful bathroom; Hong Kong couture beyond that. (If your current wardrobe is somewhat lacking in the latter, neutral silks, linens and cashmere for the city's enthusiastic air-conditioning will do.)

'Stunning views, flawless cocktails at the long bar, and Fu star-styling keep the discerning locals coming back for more.'

KOH RONG ISLANDS
CAMBODIA

Siblings don't get much lovelier than Koh Rong and its scenic sister, Koh Rong Samloem, which occupy a postcard-perfect patch in the Gulf of Thailand, off the coast of Sihanoukville. Together, they've prompted 'the new Thailand' taglines – so get there before everyone else does.

Taken on a blue-white day in high season

Song Saa Private Island

KOH RONG ISLANDS, CAMBODIA

STYLE CAMBODIAN CASTAWAY
SETTING ISLAND TWINSET

In an impossibly aquamarine patch of the Gulf of Thailand, you'll find two pristine islands lying side by side – earning them the nickname 'Song Saa' ('the sweethearts', in Khmer). Obligingly, this resort riffs on the theme of romance, seducing guests with blissfully beautiful overwater villas, seafood feasts starring bounty from the local waters, and irreproachable earth-kind credentials. If you want to lie back on its warm stretches of sand with your eyes wide shut, conscious only of the lapis lazuli-hued waters lapping the shore, that's encouraged – but guests here are also invited to join aquatic safaris and conservation activities. Start by exploring Prek Svay village on Koh Rong, where the Song Saa Foundation supports the local community.

'We head off in the speedboat and look back to find that everyone's still waving. We expected – and got – an almost ridiculous level of luxury, but hadn't counted on being quite so charmed.'

TOBY SKINNER, EDITOR IN THE EAST

THE FINER DETAILS

BEDTIME

Overwater Villa Peek at Song Saa's natural reef and its finned-and-gilled locals from the portholes of your coconut-coloured Overwater Villa, perched high above the crystalline waters. Top up your tan on the sun deck, go for a cooling dip in your private pool (or the ocean, naturally) or sit and pen some envy-inducing postcards at the writing desk. Each villa also has a sunken tub, two al fresco showers (one poolside) and an inviting lounge area. The villas take inspiration from traditional Cambodian fishing villages – but with luxurious additions, including fully stocked minibars, high-speed WiFi and Bose sound systems.

WORTH GETTING OUT OF BED FOR

Begin the day with free morning yoga, or join a meditation class at one of the hotel's immersive island locations. Forget sleeping with the fishes: here, you'll be snorkelling with them, diving with them, swimming with them and admiring them from the comfort of a sea kayak (with picnic pit stops). After dark, the bioluminescence sparkles seductively and staff will whisk you by speedboat to the best night-swimming spots. You can also embark on island safaris and have rainforest encounters with the conservation team. There are worse ways to while away 150 minutes of your life than being rubbed and scrubbed to slack-jawed nirvana, courtesy of the Song Saa Blessing spa treatment. Opt for the in-villa movie experience: staff will set up a private cinema and screen a movie of your choice – with generous supplies of on-the-house popcorn.

FOOD AND DRINK

Song Saa's Vista Restaurant sensibly acknowledges the supreme beauty of its setting by dispensing with walls, so you can continue to wonder at your surroundings over breakfast, lunch and dinner. Local fish gets star billing via dishes such as *amok* (a light, turmeric-laced curry) and *samlor kako* (a spicy soup). Kampot pepper adds a punch of flavour; other local highlights include buttery cashew nuts, creamy coconuts and wildlife-friendly Ibis rice, sourced from farmers in the north. Toast the sunset with ice-cold flutes of bubbly at the Champagne Bar, or enjoy decadent daytime libations at the relaxed Driftwood Bar.

DRESS CODE

Mangrove groove: neoprene; shells; aqua-hued wraps and shirts.

'The restaurant sensibly acknowledges the supreme beauty of its setting by dispensing with walls, so you can continue to wonder at your surroundings over breakfast, lunch and dinner.'

NISEKO JAPAN

Skiing: not synonymous with Japan, perhaps, yet the ski resort of Niseko, on Hokkaido island, proves the country is more than capable when it comes to powder-packed escapades. For liquid thrills, look to the whitewater-rapids rivers and those hot spring-speckled mountains.

Snapped between heavy winter snowfalls

Zaborin

NISEKO, JAPAN

STYLE BATHING BELLE
SETTING FAIRY-TALE FOREST

Woods can be perilous places, according to the fairy tales: visitors can easily get lost among all those trees, relying only on well-placed crumbs to find their way home again. In the depths of Hokkaido's peaceful forest, you'll find nothing so troubling: instead, a ravishing *ryokan* with 15 *onsen*-toting villas invites you in. Yes, Zaborin has its own kind of magic, but it's definitely of the white-witch kind: capacious bathtubs filled with the purest volcanic water (surely boasting healing powers); unforgettable food served with matcha tea; meadows-and-woods scenery; a nature-loving spa and the kind of quiet, heartfelt hospitality that Japan excels at.

'Once I put one leg in my *onsen*, I knew I wasn't getting out for a while. I felt the stress of 15 hours of travel melt away as I gazed upon the snow-covered forest.'

AMELIA MULARZ, US EDITOR, MR & MRS SMITH

THE FINER DETAILS

BEDTIME

Yoshitsu With Tatami Why choose between a Western-style double bed or a traditional *tatami* when you can bounce between them both? You'll wake up amid the trees, with views of Hanazono and majestic Mount Yotei from the outdoor *hinoki onsen* (and since bathing has a near-holy significance here, there's an indoor *onsen*, too). At 80 m² (860 sq ft), this villa offers the largest sleeping quarters in the house, making it a palatial treat for two. Wood, stone and slate-and-ivory hues set a calming tone; generous floor-to-ceiling windows continue the hotel's ode to the natural world. Overall, it's deliberately – and deliciously – minimalist.

WORTH GETTING OUT OF BED FOR

Stay hydrated in style by signing up for sake- and wine-tasting in the hotel's cellar. Continue the intoxicating adventure at the nearby Yoichi distillery, where you can learn all about the production – and enjoyment – of the potent Nikka whisky. Go for a wander through the Hanazono woods; if you're here in January or February, set off on a powdery adventure on Hokkaido's famous ski slopes. Honour your setting and its traditions by taking part in a Japanese tea ceremony, led by Zaborin's matcha master.

FOOD AND DRINK

Zaborin's chef returned to his Hokkaido-homeland following stints in New York and Tokyo, and his renewed romance with the region is a delicious thing to observe. The hotel offers a northern spin on traditional *kaiseki* (multi-course) dining, with an emphasis on locality and seasonality. You'll get a true taste of Hokkaido, starting with the magnificent Japanese breakfast. Potential crowd-pleasers include Rankoshi rice cooked in *kama* (traditional rice pots), pickles, milk tofu, seasonal fish, miso soup, eggs from a local farm and foil-grilled vegetables. Thirsty? Stake out seats at the 11 m (36 ft)-long counter bar, fashioned from a single piece of wood, which overlooks the hotel's private lake, the woods and Mount Yotei. You can also cosy up with drinks by the fireplace in the window-lavished lounge.

DRESS CODE

Samue robes (left for you in your room) and glowing, post-*onsen* skin.

'Unforgettable food, meadows-and-woods scenery, a nature-loving spa and the kind of quiet, heartfelt hospitality that Japan excels at.'

KRUGER NATIONAL PARK SOUTH AFRICA

This national treasure is the size of Wales – but a heck of a lot wilder. It's also one of the world's best places to spot the Big Five: lion, elephant, buffalo, leopard and rhinoceros. The park has historically provided protection for two-legged locals, too, as ancient cave paintings and Stone and Iron Age artefacts prove.

Shot as the dusts settled in December

Singita Lebombo Lodge

KRUGER NATIONAL PARK, SOUTH AFRICA

STYLE ANIMAL ATTRACTION

SETTING BY THE N'WANETSI RIVER

If you fancy roaming the Kruger National Park with the boldness and authority of a local lion, Singita Lebombo Lodge is the secluded safari retreat for you. Unlike lesser reserves, which can leave wildlife-seeking explorers feeling like they've stumbled into a tourist zoo, this private, guests-only enclave puts a patch of the park entirely at your disposal. Other feathers in its pith helmet include top-notch design, a grape-escape wine studio and an impressive choice of activities, from game drives to community visits. To help you feel at home, there is also an interactive kitchen, an espresso bar, a peaceful pool, a fleet of expert guides and a help-yourself deli (safari-ing is hungry work, after all). Last but not least, you won't get any nasty surprises at check-out: the hotel's generous rates include all food and drinks.

'"This is amazing," I thought, while snapping grazing herds. But then I returned to my room to find a net-strung, petal-strewn bed laid out under the stars and my brain couldn't settle on an adjective good enough.'

GREG FUNNELL, ADVENTURING PHOTOGRAPHER

THE FINER DETAILS

BEDTIME

Lebombo Suite Sleep suspended above the glittering N'wanetsi River in your luxe Lebombo Suite, which seems to float between the water and the sky. Inspired by the flock of eagles' nests built into the river bank, this light-filled suite glitters and glows with glass, wood, steel and natural fabrics in calming cream-and-sand shades. There's also an elevated wooden viewing deck, so keep your eyes on the prize: thirsty wildebeests and friends sauntering by for a sip. There's a romantic bed inside, but if you want to sleep beneath South African skies, with just a mosquito net separating you and the stars, you can do exactly that.

WORTH GETTING OUT OF BED FOR

Let's start with the headline act: game drives. Singita has a dream team of professional guides and trackers, plus state-of-the-art Land Rovers with space for six lucky bottoms. Even the most unobservant guest can count on spotting a wealth of wildlife, including famously large prides of lions, as well as leopards, rhinos, buffalo, elephants, hippopotamuses and cheetahs. Head out early in the morning, or join an after-dark expedition to watch nocturnal Africa at play. Alternatively, explore the park on foot, accompanied by a guide and tracker. Budding wildlife photographers can rent camera kit from the hotel, then review and edit their photos at the Photographic Library, soaking up one-on-one post-production advice from their guide. Visit the trainee chefs at the Culinary School, which supports the local community by prepping them for roles at Singita Lodges; sponsor a student if you like. Swing by the spa for a Dermalogica facial or a body treatment starring Terres d'Afrique products; post-beautification, count the twinkling stars overhead. You could even perfect your archery skills by the N'wanetsi River.

FOOD AND DRINK

This is your chance to sample (if your conscience permits) some of the birds and beasts you've admired on safari; ostrich, antelope, kudu, blesbok and springbok all grace the menu. For an Attenborough-worthy setting in which to enjoy them, ask staff to arrange dinner *à deux* in the bush, replete with flickering hurricane lamps, your own private chef and a *banakeli* (butler). Thanks to the efforts of its star sommelier, the hotel aces wine. Have a personalized tasting in the lodge's temperature-controlled cellar (the wine studio also has a library, a multimedia room and a rooftop viewing area). Thirsty explorers will no doubt appreciate the minibar, stocked with sparkling water, South African wine and a bottle of *amarula*: a creamy, fruity local liqueur.

DRESS CODE

Robert Redford and Meryl Streep in *Out of Africa* are your inspirations here: loose linens, cappuccino-and-caramel hues, safari-swept hair.

'This private, guests-only enclave puts a patch of the park entirely at your disposal.'

ROME ITALY

Few cities have inspired the devotion prompted by this sensuous capital, which has stirred the imagination of Raphael, Michelangelo and millions of Vatican-visiting worshippers. Traverse centuries in mere footsteps: Rome's streets, sites and sights bear ancient, medieval and modern imprints.

Shot while the artichokes bloomed, ready to grace Roman plates

JK Place Roma

ROME, ITALY

STYLE CLASSICAL CIVILIZATION
SETTING HISTORIC CENTRO STORICO

Here at JK Roma, beautiful Italians in various states of undress pose casually in all their nubile glory in the communal areas (before you blush, they're classical statues). Jewel-box colours, mid-century furniture and generous servings of marble, velvet, gold and glass add to the Euro-flash eye candy. A hotel set in Rome's former school of architecture is honour-bound to do its setting justice; luckily, top-of-the-class designer Michele Bönan (the man behind Roma's JK sisters in Capri and Florence) orchestrated its styling. The location is equally *bella donna* – though the taffeta-bedecked restaurant, wood-panelled bar and romantic rooms might distract you from exploring. Brunch-addicts: it's worth hopping out of bed for the superb Sunday marathon of homemade bread and pastries, regional meats and cheeses, traditional pasta dishes, and tiramisu.

'Simple, modern, elegant, luxurious. Every single detail is designed with a subtlety that as a whole – like Rome itself – is overwhelmingly gorgeous. It is an all-encompassing experience of perfection.'

MATTHEW MALIN, SKINCARE SAGE

THE FINER DETAILS

BEDTIME

Master Room Set in what was once a classroom used by budding architectural talent, these sleeping quarters deliver a sartorial masterclass in Italian sophistication. Expect bespoke furniture designed by Michele Bönan himself, a handsome rosewood four-poster bed, an emperor-worthy marble bathroom and a snug sitting area. The shower is on the pleasingly large side, the Italian minibar snacks and soft drinks are on the house, and super-soft bathrobes and slippers await inside the walk-in closets. Don't worry if you forgot your Kindle: the Master Room has a tempting stash of tomes, too.

WORTH GETTING OUT OF BED FOR

Brush up on Renaissance masters in the cosy library, before heading out to see their proudest achievements in the flesh. Modern-art lovers will love Maxxi, the national museum of 21st-century art. If you're a fan of the classical sculptures that ornament JK Roma, admire more of the same at Palazzo Altemps, just across from Piazza Navona. A smorgasbord of Rome's must-see sights are all within easy reach: start with the Spanish Steps, the Trevi Fountain and Pantheon, all within a 10-minute walk. Nearby, Via Condotti provides a who's who of Italian fashion; invest in all things logoed and monogrammed at Gucci, Prada, Ferragamo and Bulgari. The English-style Villa Borghese gardens are decorated with cooling lakes and flower-scented shaded spots, perfect for resting post-shopping feet; once you've recovered, meander up the gravel paths to glorious art-filled Renaissance villas.

FOOD AND DRINK

Proving that the word 'café' isn't always synonymous with frill-free, Formica-topped tables, regrettable vinyl flooring and utilitarian tableware, JKCafe woos eyes and appetites alike. Walls are dressed in pops of saffron, chartreuse and teal, providing a colourful setting for the market-fresh Med dishes. The JK Burger (a holy trinity of Piedmont beef, Tuscan bacon and Italian cheese) has a loyal fan base, but it would be a shame to miss the local-loving options, too. Try the pork-cheeky carbonara, or *cacio e pepe* enlivened with smoked cardamom powder, perhaps. Breakfast is a generous spread; don't miss the chef's surprise '*buongiorno*' of the day. JKCafe Bar is a Fifties-fabulous vision of vintage photography, abstract onyx sculptures and glittering brass; slink here for some icy prosecco or a JK sour: a zingy blend of Amaretto, passion fruit and lemon.

DRESS CODE

Audrey and Gregory in *Roman Holiday*: feminine silhouettes accessorized with a gelato and a gamine fringe for the Mrs; nonchalant tailoring for our would-be Pecks. (If in doubt, consult the local heroes: Fendi, Giambattista Valli, vintage Schiaparelli.)

'Jewel-box colours, mid-century furniture and generous servings of marble, velvet, gold and glass add to the Euro-flash eye candy.'

BAHIA BRAZIL

As intoxicating as the local caipirinhas, Bahia is a natural-born thriller, where glittering coastlines collide with desert-like landscapes. Historic architecture hints at the area's colonial past; flamboyant carnivals reveal its enduring fun side.

Shot in the presence of a local pineapple-vendor (and his trusty steed)

Uxua Casa Hotel & Spa

BAHIA, BRAZIL

STYLE TRIBUTE TO TRANCOSO
SETTING THE COLOURFUL QUADRADO

It's not hard to imagine the glee that Portuguese explorer Pedro Álvares Cabral must have felt when he washed up on the shores of Trancoso back in 1500. Today, come-hither beaches and the UNESCO-listed Quadrado – the historic, car-free main square, with an all-white, 16th-century church and clusters of crayon-bright houses – continue to lure modern-day explorers, many of whom jet over in winter, fleeing colder climes. Bronzed Brazilian supermodels, off-duty A-listers and the jet-set cognoscenti all flit like human butterflies to this ravishing Bahian landmark; Uxua Casa Hotel & Spa is the one and only boutique hotel in the Quadrado. Lucky visitors share it with friendly groups of football-crazy Brazilian boys; join them for an impromptu match on one of their makeshift pitches.

'We awake to beams of sunlight, the heady scent of the rainforest and the clamour of insects and birds. Then we retrace our steps to the beach – a swim here, a snooze there, such is life.'

LAYO PASKIN, DJ-TURNED-RESTAURATEUR

THE FINER DETAILS

BEDTIME

Casa da Árvore Uxua Casa has serious sartorial *cajones*: it's designed and owned by Wilbert Das – former creative director of Italian label Diesel – and his high-flying partner, Bob Shevlin (also ex-Diesel). This dream team's combined eye for design sparkles throughout their innovative eco-triumph, and is particularly apparent in the lofty Casa da Árvore, a three-level Bahian treehouse fashioned from toffee-coloured recycled wood. Decorated with bright-white furnishings, the cosy Casa has a thatched roof, a covered veranda with a hammock and bar area, a double shower in the bathroom and a spa tub on the outdoor deck – as well as a swing underneath for those Tarzan moments.

WORTH GETTING OUT OF BED FOR

Cool off in the main pool, shaped like a mini lake and constructed from thousands of green aventurine stones. Alternatively, laze on the hotel's stretch of beach or hit the semi-deserted stretches of sand: Praia dos Nativos, Praia dos Coqueiros, Praia da Pedra Grande and Praia do Espelho. Have a treatment at the Almescar Spa, home to Bahia's first Vichy treatment suite, where warm water pours down from carved eucalyptus trunks. Request a guided horseback ride along the beach, or go mountain biking through forests thick with mangrove trees. Lessons in *capoeira* (a mix of music, dance and martial arts) and *forró* are held in the hotel's studio, or book an hour-long session with local champs at the cultural centre. Go kayaking or surfing; embark on a tour of nearby Caraíva village and the Aldeia Pataxó reservation; hop on a boat to more beaches (ask nicely and your captain will drop anchor by a reef). You could also zip out for a day on the hotel's speedboat.

FOOD AND DRINK

Uxua Casa's relaxed-to-horizontal approach to life extends to its restaurant, which doesn't have a formal moniker (and doesn't need one, since its dishes speak for themselves). Sample Brazilian classics that take their cues from their surroundings: 'fisherman's spaghetti'; lobster and king-prawn *moqueca*, or meat, cassava and coconut-milk *escondidinho* (a Brazilian take on shepherd's pie). You can also borrow one of the private chefs and ask them to cook a feast for two, to be enjoyed in the comfort of your casa – or on the beach. The restaurant serves drinks, but the champion spot for cocktails is the bossa nova-loving beach bar, which rustles up pineapple-and-ginger caipirinhas till sundown. A former boat serves as the drinks counter – honour its nautical past by imbibing rum in piratical proportions.

DRESS CODE

Cool and casual as you like – if you modelled PJs, nobody would bat an eyelid. Trancoso has a hippie past, so loosen those buttons and free your toes.

'The champion spot for cocktails is the bossa nova-loving beach bar, which rustles up pineapple-and-ginger caipirinhas till sundown.'

KANGAROO ISLAND
AUSTRALIA

The centuries-old shipwrecks around Australia's third-largest island are testament to its siren-like qualities. Awash with wowing wilderness, it's a place where life happens at a gentle pace – for humans, kangaroos or any other inhabitant.

Photographed under the fiery February sky

Southern Ocean Lodge

KANGAROO ISLAND, AUSTRALIA

STYLE WILD AT HEART
SETTING AUSTRALIA'S GALAPAGOS

If you lifted up Noah's Ark and (gently) emptied out its contents onto an untouched Australian island, you'd come close to Southern Ocean Lodge's sensational setting and its finned, feathered and four-legged locals. Instead of flood waters, the hotel is surrounded by the crystalline expanse of the Great Australian Bight; and instead of Noah and sons, there's a team of obliging staff and animal experts on hand to introduce you to the region's flora and fauna. More than a third of Kangaroo Island is protected by nature reserves; to the west, the sea-sculpted Remarkable Rocks and black-tie penguin colonies await. Continue the local education of your tastebuds by indulging at the Lodge's deliciously Down Under restaurant, perhaps after one or two spa treatments starring indigenous Australian botanicals.

'It feels like we've found *the* perfect escape from the bustling
city. It's completely serene, has the most wonderful sense of place
and everything goes above and beyond – from the inspired menus
to the admirable eco-efforts.'

LOUISE OLSEN AND STEPHEN ORMANDY, DESIGNER DUO

THE FINER DETAILS

BEDTIME

Osprey Pavilion There's room enough for all creatures great and small to bed down in the eye-popping Osprey Pavilion – but they might get in the way of the sunken lounge with its open fire and high-tech audio-visual system. Mother Nature lays on plenty of audio-visual treats of her own, to be fair – they're best witnessed from your outdoor terrace and private plunge spa. For additional pruney-skinned moments, there's a freestanding bath shaped like a giant egg, hewn from stone and positioned in full view of the windows. See if you can make a kangaroo blush ...

WORTH GETTING OUT OF BED FOR

This is your chance to wave hello to wallabies, echidnas, possums, koalas, goannas, New Zealand fur seals, sea lions, and more; Flinders Chase and Kelly Hill national parks offer a wealth of animal-watching activities. Borrow mountain bikes and set off exploring, or sign up for a private-charter tour around the island. Cast your fishing line at tranquil Hanson Bay – come dinner time, ask the hotel's handy chefs to grill your catch to perfection for you. The hotel's lobby alone merits a holiday: the bar and restaurant occupy a large part of it, but there's also a walk-in wine cellar, a shop selling local wares, a sunken lounge area with a *très bon* French fireplace suspended from the ceiling, racks of offbeat books and hip magazines, and an outdoor extension with a plunge pool. What's better than kangaroos and koalas? Kangaroos, koalas, canapés and champagne, of course: the hotel's sunset Kangas & Kanapés session delivers just that.

FOOD AND DRINK

Discover South Australia's glut of gluttonously good produce, game, fish and seafood (including superstar southern rock lobster) by hopping from dish to dish with help from the five-course tasting menus and four-course à la carte feasts. Dishes are determined by the seasons; previous crowd-pleasers include local queen snapper, king-crab salad, and house-made gnocchi with samphire. Kangaroo Island is home to the world's one and only population of pure-bred, disease-free Ligurian honey bees: slather KI honey on your breakfast toast with wild abandon. Tuck in: rates include all your food and drink (plus select activities and transfers). On the topic of imbibing, the open-plan bar in the panoramic Great Room is a scenic setting in which to raise a toast.

DRESS CODE

Billionaire botanist: outfits that will take you from island safaris to sundowners.

'There's a freestanding bath shaped like a giant egg, hewn from stone and positioned in full view of the windows. See if you can make a kangaroo blush ...'

HAMPSHIRE UK

The birthplace of Jane Austen, Hampshire continues to over-deliver on textbook English charm: from the pony-packed forests – where ye olde free-grazing rights still rule OK – to the county's characterful pubs, peaceful picnic spots and cream-dream tea rooms.

Shot as the autumn berries ripened

Chewton Glen

HAMPSHIRE, UK

STYLE SPA-SPANGLED MANOR

SETTING NESTLED IN THE NEW FOREST

Oh Chewton, you champion – if it wasn't so un-British, we'd shout from the treetops about our ardent love for you. (It's more elegant to write a love letter instead, so here goes.) This stately Georgian manor and cosmopolitan country club has a ravishingly regal demeanour, a spoiling spa, a wow-factor restaurant, a holiday's worth of outdoor pursuits and utterly gorgeous grounds in which to enjoy them. Best of all, its serious levels of luxury also come with a generous dose of humour and charm – as evidenced by the decidedly un-straightlaced Treehouse retreats. NB: If you want to arrive by chopper – and frankly, who doesn't? – call ahead: there's only space for three at a time on the helipad.

'The bed is bigger than my whole bedroom at home, the secluded balcony has the most incredible view, the carpet is toe-sinkingly thick and there's a whole wall of mirrored wardrobes. This is pure, unadulterated sumptuousness.'

HELEN MCNUTT, JOURNEYING JOURNALIST

THE FINER DETAILS

BEDTIME

Treehouse Hideaway Suite Chewton's suites deliver Tarzan-and-Jane highs (if Tarzan had gone to Eton and Lady Jane had boarded at Cheltenham Ladies' College). Near-hidden by greenery and fringed by foliage, these circular nests float high up in the leafy canopy; take in the sweeping views from your private deck. (Add to the scenery by stripping off for the al fresco hot tub.) The marshmallow-soft carpet, wood-burning stove and toasty underfloor heating mean you'll be as snug as a bug in a rug. Additional cues for your birthday suits include the marble-floored en suite and its freestanding bath with forest views – plus that tempting bed. You won't have to do anything as pedestrian as walking: breakfast hampers are delivered daily, and there's a regular shuttle service to whisk you to and from the main building.

WORTH GETTING OUT OF BED FOR

Don't go home without having a game of croquet (there are tennis courts and a nine-hole golf course to tackle, too). The terrace plays host to afternoon tea in fine weather, or hone your pâtisserie skills at The Kitchen Cookery School, where classes range from chocolate-crafting to sessions with celebrity chefs. Make like the landed gentry by indulging in clay-pigeon shooting, archery or gun-dog herding; for something a little more playful, sign up for a treasure hunt or a spot of off-road buggy-racing. Book yourselves in for *kundalini* massages in one of the couple's treatment rooms at the Spa, whose merits include Europe's largest hydrotherapy pool, aromatherapy saunas, crystal steam rooms and an outdoor whirlpool. Nautical-types: ask the hotel to arrange luxury yacht charters or sailing trips at nearby Lymington. The seaside is just a stroll away; take a Chewton-prepped picnic with you.

FOOD AND DRINK

Acknowledging that croquet-ing, shooting, spa-ing and good old-fashioned loving are hungry work, Chewton Glen boasts a five-roomed gastrodome called The Dining Room. Ingredients for the award-winning, fine-dining dishes are sourced from the hotel's own kitchen garden. For something a little more casual, visit the open-plan Kitchen, where you can watch nimble-knuckled chefs rustle up wood-fired pizzas, gourmet burgers, superfood salads, and more. You won't want to leave, but chip butties and champagne at the Beachcomber Café in Barton on Sea are as good a reason as any. Return for brandies at Vetiver, the plummy-hued, leather-lavished, gentlemen's club-style bar.

DRESS CODE

Best of British: a bit of Barbour, Aquascutum and subtle Burberry. Tailored togs for the Mr, jewels and lace for the Mrs, cashmere and cologne for both.

'Near-hidden by greenery and fringed by foliage, these circular nests float high up in the leafy canopy; take in the sweeping views from your private deck.'

PARIS FRANCE

A metaphorical *macaron* for the soul, this cultured charmer
built by the ancient Romans (it was called Lutetia back then)
woos with its tree-lined boulevards, bistros by the *douzaine*,
Gothic architecture, a cloud-poking Tower and a few
hush-hush romantic surprises.

Photographed as the leaves fell in Paris's parks

Le Roch Hotel & Spa

PARIS, FRANCE

STYLE PARISIAN BOMBSHELL

SETTING STEPS FROM LE LOUVRE

During the Belle Époque, Moulin Rouge set Parisian pulses racing, as artists and poets fraternized with ladies of the night and can-can frenzies of black stockings, bare legs, lacy knickers and thigh-high kicks had audiences gagging for more. The City of Lights still knows all there is to know about the art of seduction, as Le Roch Hotel & Spa so emphatically proves (though, admittedly, more quietly and with a lot less spectacle). This 19th-century charmer also has a few tricks left up its sleeve: a secret terrace; a rare-for-Paris pool (candlelit and carved from black lava rock, no less); a hammam accessed via a waterfall; a Codage spa; a sublime, refined restaurant – and that's just for starters.

'Ahhh, the bedroom – or rather, the indulgence room. Did I mention it comes with a hammam? Beyond the his-and-hers sinks is a glass door leading to a Moroccan-tiled wet room that, sure enough, moonlights as a hammam.'

AUDREY WARD, HOTEL-LOVING EDITOR

THE FINER DETAILS

BEDTIME

Saint-Roch Suite Parisian designer Sarah Lavoine has lavished Le Roch with Gallic good taste: rooms are kitted out with Carrara marble, walnut floors, furniture by Cassina and GamFratesi and Chevalier Edition carpets; bathrooms, on the other hand, have Kaldewei tubs and colourful Moroccan *zelliges* (handmade clay tiles). The style stakes climax in the penthouse Saint-Roch Suite. Four words guaranteed to please: 'private in-room hammam'. Yup, the suite has one, but it doesn't stop there – a balcony surveys the courtyard and city vistas unfold from the windows; on a clear day you can see the bronze statue of Napoleon atop his column in the Place Vendôme. There's also a cavernous dressing area, a free minibar and a well-stocked wine bar. *Ooh la la!*

WORTH GETTING OUT OF BED FOR

You're likely to have a devilishly good time inside the hotel's pool and spa, but be sure to head outside, too, since Le Roch's near neighbours are blockbuster sights and smash-hit attractions. The Palais-Royal, Place du Marché Saint-Honoré, Place Vendôme, Opéra and the Louvre are all an easy 10-minute walk away. So too is the regal Tuileries Garden, primed for a promenade with stops at the Musée de l'Orangerie (for Monet's *Water Lilies*), Jeu de Paume (for postmodern photography) or, of course, the Louvre (for that enigmatic smile and much, much more). Cross the Seine to explore the Beaux Arts station-turned-gallery Musée d'Orsay, or mooch around the Marais. Shoppers: cherry-pick luxury boutiques on Rue Saint-Honoré or treasure-hunt for antiques in the ornate *passages couverts*. Alternatively, snuggle up by the crackling fire in Le Roch's erudite library.

FOOD AND DRINK

Executive chef Rémy Bererd is the man behind the menus here, and the accomplished, elegant cuisine showcases his playful way with texture and flavour: expect creative pairings that will have you smiling before you've even sampled them. (If you're genuinely spoilt for choice, the veal with candied-lemon gnocchi and fried capers is one of Rémy's culinary signatures.) Thanks to Lavoine, the setting is equally tasty: blush-pink and teal velvet chairs; glittering gold and lust-worthy tableware. Post-meal, roll yourselves over to Le Roch's small-but-smashing bar for at least one On The Roch: a zingy mash-up of vodka, rum and herbal Galliano liqueur with tropical fruit juices.

DRESS CODE

Remember the immortal words of Coco Chanel: 'Simplicity is the keynote of true elegance.' (More ominously, she also declared: 'A women who doesn't wear perfume has no future.')

'A balcony surveys the courtyard and city vistas unfold from the windows; on a clear day you can see the bronze statue of Napoleon atop his column in the Place Vendôme.'

PIGEON BAY
NEW ZEALAND

Cleaving inland, the emerald waters of Pigeon Bay lap velvety rolling hills, reflecting wide-open skies. You won't spot any hobbits (or their diminutive houses) here, but you will find working farms, migrating whales and the occasional bit of arresting architecture.

Shot while the local grapes dangled plumply from the vines

Annandale

PIGEON BAY, NEW ZEALAND

STYLE KIWI BEAUT
SETTING CINEMATIC PIGEON BAY

We're not normally in the habit of envying seed-eating birds, but things changed when we discovered Pigeon Bay, named by whalers for its vast numbers of Columbidae. The bay is a remote, rugged patch of coastal Kiwi perfection – so remote it helps to have a chopper to get here – and Annandale is an additional feather in its cap. This handsome hotel (and working farm) set along the Banks Peninsula, on the South Island's eastern coast, has four private villas, including a futuristic couple's escape and a 19th-century clapboard-clad homestead. Each has its own untamed style and windswept setting; flawless service, eye-bogglingly beautiful scenery, adrenalin-rush activities and handy resident chefs unite the quartet.

'As cosy as it comes for couples: heated floors, a super-king bed, fireplaces inside and out, and a hanging sheepskin bubble chair with movie-villain views of the bay, where you can't help but lose track of time.'

TAMARA LOHAN, THE ORIGINAL MRS SMITH

THE FINER DETAILS

BEDTIME

Seascape Frolicking seals and gambolling dolphins are your only neighbours at Seascape, a glittering glass residence that shimmers and sparkles like the private bay below it. This minimalist love nest has a king-size bed on a raised dais (all the better to see those waves from); other Pacific Coast-viewing points include a spacious deck and a bathroom with an arrow-slit window that lets guests admire the sea while bathing. A turf roof and stone walls help the villa blend into its sensational setting; for more manmade moments, there's a TV with DVD player, an iPod dock, WiFi and Sonos entertainment system. An on-loan private chef will happily work wonders in the modern-marvel kitchen, which has everything you need – and then some.

WORTH GETTING OUT OF BED FOR

Annandale has over 4,000 acres to explore – and pushing 4,000 ways in which to enjoy them. Start with a guided 4x4 tour, admiring the shearers in action and waving hello to the working sheepdogs en route. Go hiking or biking – the Pigeon Bay Walkway, a 14-km (9-mile) adventure, is a good place to start – or sign up for a cookery class. Guides will take you kayaking or on an expedition in a powerboat, so that you can spot friendly Hector's dolphins, fur seals, blue penguins and bird colonies. The French-influenced town of Akaroa is a half-hour drive away; head there for day cruises, fishing and diving trips, penguin-spotting adventures, water-skiing, sea-kayaking, jet-boating, and more. Alternatively, make like a pigeon and take to the skies: a chopper tour will give you a bird's-eye view of your surroundings.

FOOD AND DRINK

Acknowledging that guests won't want to step far from their villa, Pigeon Bay's private chef will orchestrate culinary symphonies from the comfort of Seascape. If you'd like to be more independent when it comes to eating arrangements, swap the chef for the clever 'we create, you serve' system. Breakfast, a hamper-packed picnic lunch and a three-course dinner will be delivered to your villa daily – along with instructions on how to prepare them. (You'll have been carefully quizzed on your food preferences long before you've even got here.)

DRESS CODE

Leather, wool and windswept hair.

'Annandale has over 4,000 acres to explore – and pushing 4,000 ways in which to enjoy them.'

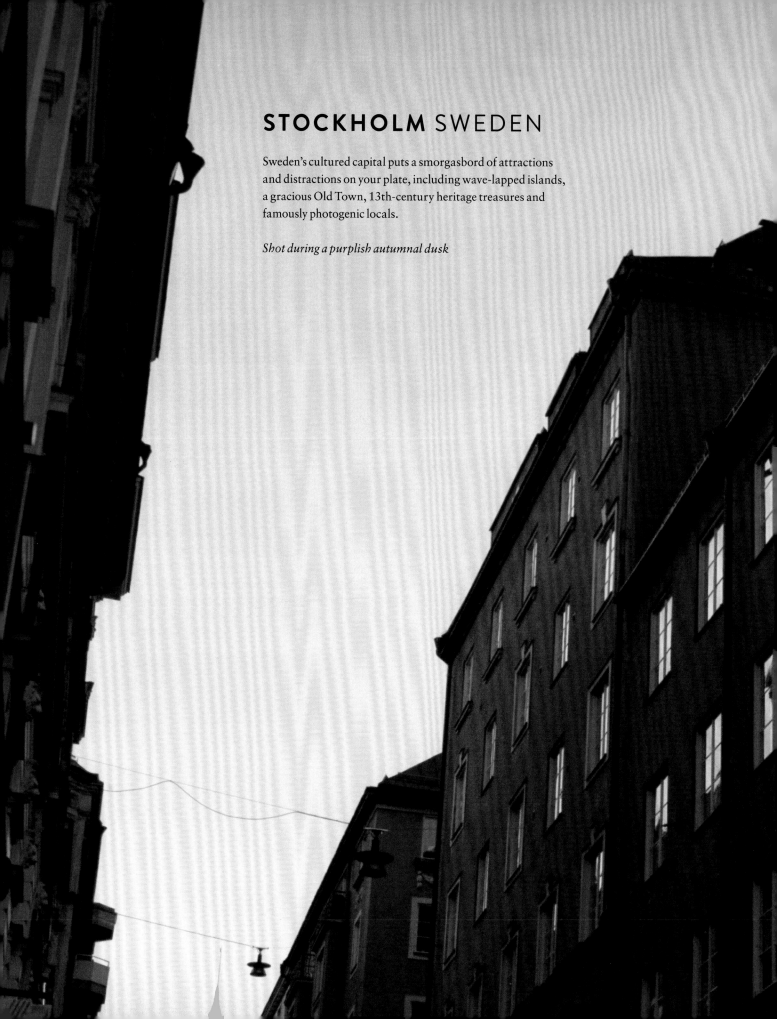

STOCKHOLM SWEDEN

Sweden's cultured capital puts a smorgasbord of attractions and distractions on your plate, including wave-lapped islands, a gracious Old Town, 13th-century heritage treasures and famously photogenic locals.

Shot during a purplish autumnal dusk

Ett Hem

STOCKHOLM, SWEDEN

STYLE COURTESY OF ILSE CRAWFORD
SETTING LEAFY LÄRKSTADEN

Mirror, mirror on the wall, who is the fairest of them all? When in Stockholm, the answer has to be Ett Hem: a diminutive darling in a green and peaceful 'hood. This supremely stylish stay is the work of discerning owner Jeanette Mix and world-famous interior designer Ilse Crawford (of Babington House fame). The partnership has yielded delicious fruit: the made-for-*Monocle* rooms are decorated with vintage curios, jelly-coloured glass ornaments, glittering brass and chic Michael Anastassiades lights. It's triumphantly easy on the eyes, but Ett Hem works magic on the soul, too: its name means 'at home' in Swedish (but we think this is a little modest). Guests are invited to treat the place – and the just-baked sponge cakes – as their own; meals are arranged around their tastes and timings; and the service is relaxed, personal and utterly charming. If this really was our home, we'd never leave.

'These are not rooms of snotty grandeur, but of calm
and gentle loveliness. There really is a genuine sense of
homeliness here – albeit of the eye-flirtingly tasteful kind.'

TOM JEFFREYS, ART-LOVING WRITER

THE FINER DETAILS

BEDTIME

The Suite Ett Hem might just be at its loveliest in the seductive Suite, with its sunny colour scheme courtesy of a yolk-yellow rug and matching curtains (which, when flung back, reveal prime Stockholm views). Avoid the temptation to take home the vintage chandelier and equally covetable massive marble bathtub (handily positioned by the corner windows). Items to distract you from city explorations include the majestic four-poster bed, copper-clad bathroom and swellegant dining area. Everybody knows that *lagom* is the new *hygge*: up your *lagom*-game by stoking the flames (metaphorical or otherwise) with help from the Suite's tiled bedside stove.

WORTH GETTING OUT OF BED FOR

What could be more Swedish than a spot of sauna time? Ett Hem has a basement steam-dream tricked out with a slab of hot stone to relax on, plus a shriek-inducing pull-down bucket of ice-cold water (so good for the circulation, darling); guests can also request a massage or beauty treatment featuring fragrant Kiehl's products. Scandi-up your wardrobe by heading to Bibliotekstan, lined with swish boutiques stocked with cutting-edge Scandinavian labels. Dreams (of the edible, *smørrebrød* kind) come true at Östermalms Saluhall, a lavish 1880s food hall where a bounty of delicacies vie for your tastebuds' attention. Go for a wander along the waterfront, admiring the city's gingerbread-house architecture, particularly Bünsow House on Strandvägen: a visual feast of turrets, dormers and brick.

FOOD AND DRINK

In keeping with its Swedish home-from-home feel, Ett Hem doesn't have a formal restaurant – it has a relaxed kitchen. The friendly chefs devise the day's menu each morning, but guests are also encouraged to put in any requests and to help themselves to snacks whenever hunger strikes (though you'll regret spoiling your appetite when you see dinner). The menus champion local produce; you could be nibbling gingerbread with truffled foie gras, artichoke with roe, or veal tartare with sturgeon caviar. Eat wherever you like: at the kitchen table; in the pretty, plant-stuffed conservatory or peaceful library; at the sociable dining table. Breakfast is an impressive spread of cheese, cold cuts, pastries, and more, with hot options on offer, too; the daily on-the-house cake, eaten warm from the oven, is another highlight. Rustle up your favourite cocktails at the brass honesty bar, whose pull-out shelves are laden with every conceivable flute, coupe and highball.

DRESS CODE

Nordic whimsy: delicate floral prints and silks for summer; knitwear worthy of Sarah Lund or Eva Thörnblad come winter. NB: A light rain jacket will stand you in good stead while you're gadding about Stockholm.

'What could be more Swedish than a spot of sauna time? Ett Hem has a basement steam-dream tricked out with a slab of hot stone to relax on.'

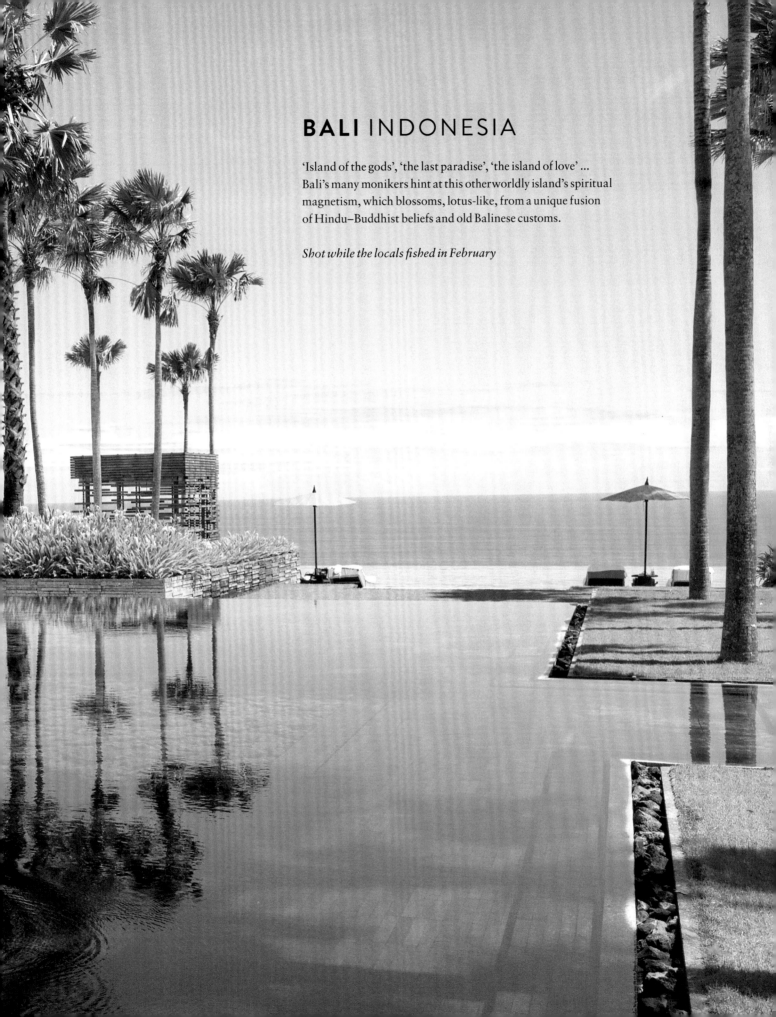

BALI INDONESIA

'Island of the gods', 'the last paradise', 'the island of love' ...
Bali's many monikers hint at this otherworldly island's spiritual
magnetism, which blossoms, lotus-like, from a unique fusion
of Hindu–Buddhist beliefs and old Balinese customs.

Shot while the locals fished in February

Alila Villas Uluwatu

BALI, INDONESIA

STYLE EAT, STAY, LOVE
SETTING INDIAN OCEAN CLIFFTOP

Levitating takes practice – but walking on cloud nine is inevitable at Alila Villas Uluwatu, a celestially serene retreat on the Bukit Peninsula. The hotel's cliffside perch doesn't exactly detract from the fallen-from-heaven feel, nor do the spa's fleet of miracle-working masseuses or the flock of speak-and-ye-shall-find butlers (set your preferred service level to 'private', 'discreet' or 'indulgent'). The 'whoa'-worthy design comes courtesy of trailblazing Singapore architects WOHA; the incredible views and scenery are all down to Mother Nature. It would be easy to unwind to the point of horizontal at all times here, but you might want to wake up every now and then to check for any monkey business: those furry, four-legged locals do rather like to 'borrow' things.

'The whole world feels mere steps from your bed, yet as far
away as humanly possible. It's a fine line between intimacy
and isolation – this hotel threads the needle perfectly.'

DAVID WEINER, MEDIA TRAILBLAZER

THE FINER DETAILS

BEDTIME

One-Bedroom Villa With Pool What do you mean you've never bedded down in a Balinese pool villa with a bamboo ceiling, lava-rock roof, outdoor dining area and relaxation cabana overlooking the Indian Ocean? Change all that at Alila's pool-graced One-Bedroom Villa, which boasts an eco-conscious, open-plan layout and an abundance of soothing sea breezes. Wood, stone and rattan tell the sartorial story; there's also a tempting king-size bed and a bodacious bathroom with a bathtub and indoor–outdoor rain and jet showers. *Namaste*.

WORTH GETTING OUT OF BED FOR

A lie down by the infinity pool, which appears to float on high above the Indian Ocean, counts as an activity here. (Livelier types can canter down the hotel's 100 or so steps to the private beach; you'll certainly have earned your sandside somnolence by the time you arrive.) Sign up for a Journey By Alila experience to explore the region: you could visit a noteworthy Balinese artist, take a trip to the fishmarket, or have an Indonesian cookery class. The rugged Bukit Peninsula is salty catnip for surfers, so have a lesson while you're here. Learn about Balinese culture at the cliff-hugging, black-coral Uluwatu Temple, next to the hotel and believed by locals to guard the island. Achieve literal and spiritual balance by trying stand-up paddleboard yoga in the infinity pool. Stay on a high at the signature spa, which lives up to Alila's unrivalled reputation, wellness-wise. How's about the Blissful Spa Indulgence? This two-hour ritual kicks off with a footbath and proceeds to a warm oil massage and Shirodhara (hot oils are poured onto the forehead to wash away your worries), before culminating with a herbal bath and servings of fresh coconut water.

FOOD AND DRINK

There's a holy trinity of restaurants here: Western-style Cire, whose dishes pay tribute to their sea-sprayed surroundings (wasabi crab, roasted king prawns, grilled octopus); relaxed Warung, which aces authentic Indonesian flavours in its comforting concoctions; and Med-inspired Quila, which does whizzy things with local produce in its imaginative dishes (try the carrot curry).

DRESS CODE

Lapsed-angel chic: ethereal white layers and a zen demeanour (with a hint of sauciness).

'A lie down by the infinity pool, which appears to float on high above the Indian Ocean, counts as an activity here.'

LONDON UK

Percy Bysshe Shelley called this urban playground a 'great sea'; to Benjamin Disraeli, it was a 'modern Babylon' and 'a roost for every bird'. Despite every effort to pin it down, London's capital character continues to defy categorization.

Captured while winter snuck in uninvited

The Franklin

LONDON, UK

STYLE BLACK PEARL
SETTING SWELLEGANT SW3

'I really should have been a pharaoh, do you know that?' So spoke Anouska Hempel – aka Lady Weinberg – the model, actress, Bond girl and world-famous designer behind Blakes, The Franklin, and a clutch of other desirable stays. The Franklin catches the glamorous, globetrotting designer in an Italian state of mind: its darkly decadent interiors pay tribute to the Duomo in Milan and the Doge's Palace in Venice. The Roman-holiday seduction continues in the va-va-voom rooms and restaurant; Istanbul gets a look in, too, thanks to monochrome ikat cushions and a diminutive hammam. Instead of postcards from France, a botanist-pleasing array of vintage Gallic pressed plants are displayed like natural artworks in Hempel's signature more-is-more arrangements.

'I feel far from home in the best possible sense. Every convenience is at my fingertips – in the most luxurious iterations: crisp Frette bedlinen, the fluffiest of bathrobes, quality minibar snacks ripe for splurging on.'

ROSA PARK, *CEREAL* TRAVELLER

THE FINER DETAILS

BEDTIME

The Presidential Suite In The Franklin's Presidential Suite, things get a little *50 Shades of Grey* – when it comes to the colour scheme, that is. Walls are covered in moodily magnificent paper, with roughly textured puffs of clouds floating across them; glass, velvet-upholstered furniture and silk curtains riff on different hues of charcoal, pewter, steel and silver. The effect is palatial: throw in glittering, gold-accented coffee tables and Brompton Oratory views, and it's so luxurious, you almost need a lie-down. Luckily, there's a giant four-poster bed (with the most majestic mirrored headboard you'll ever make eyes at), plus a high-spec Italian-sandstone bathroom with an ink-black bathtub and a stash of Penhaligon's unguents and marshmallow-soft bathrobes.

WORTH GETTING OUT OF BED FOR

You could practically hop out of bed and straight into the neoclassical Brompton Oratory: step inside to admire its opulent architecture up close. Heritage heavyweights are ten-a-penny on your doorstep: tick off South Kensington's multiple museums and galleries (the V&A is a short stroll away); flex your plastic athletically at Harrods and Harvey Nicks. At the hotel itself, squirrel yourself away in the milk-white library with a tome or two, test out the top-notch equipment in the mini-gym and get your glow on in the hammam. On sunny days, sit in Egerton Gardens (tea/G&T in hand) and befriend the resident lords and ladies who share their prime patch of London's open space with the hotel. On date night, seek out some silver-screen romance at the local Art Deco Ciné Lumière. Having explored your hero 'hood, hop on the Tube to central London for a change of pace and more city kicks. Start at Sir John Soane's Museum, where you can appraise the architect's drawings, paintings and curios.

FOOD AND DRINK

The Franklin's bar has a crush on that most English of libations: gin. Pick from more than 22 varieties, many of which are showcased in inventive seasonal cocktails. You know you're in safe hands when a bar boasts a mini-flotilla of vermouths and bitters housed in vintage perfume bottles, ready to be spritzed on command. Talking of safe hands, Italian culinary talent Alfredo Russo is responsible for the dishes served in the velvet-lavished restaurant. There are some pizazzy antipasti – octopus comes with Piedmont potato foam; *tartaccio* is topped with lemon caramel – but the mains are reassuringly hearty. Highlights include exemplary *cacio e pepe*, steamed sea bass with onion and basil, and hen *tortelli* with Parmesan fondue and lime zest.

DRESS CODE

Capri via Kensington: cashmere, velvet and zhuzhy tailoring.

'Darkly decadent interiors pay tribute to the Duomo in Milan and the Doge's Palace in Venice.'

TURKS & CAICOS ISLANDS CARIBBEAN

Beautiful enough to distract a pirate from his doubloons –
and unofficial winner of 'The Least British Part of Britain'
award – these 40 sun-kissed islands are home to dolphins,
flamingos, honeymooners and rightfully proud locals (the
self-titled 'Belongers').

Shot while the humpback whales swam south

Como Parrot Cay

TURKS & CAICOS ISLANDS, CARIBBEAN

STYLE COMO CASTAWAY
SETTING PRIVATE-ISLAND IDYLL

Your average treasure island can only be accessed via a parchment map; we much prefer Como's approach. Guests just need to fly to Providenciales International Airport, where the hotel's unflappable staff will meet you, greet you and whisk you off by boat to your new favourite place in the world. Located on a formerly wild, uninhabited island, this Caribbean dream-stay is set on a tiny atoll, with a tranquil mangrove lagoon and a mile of unspoilt, uninhabited and unforgettable beach. Distinguished fans of this tropical treat include a certain follically challenged actor and a swimsuit-sporting model – both of whom have wisely invested (separately) in its butler-equipped estates. In the absence of a superstar bank balance, you too can have a piece of the treasure, by booking a suspended-reality stay in one of the VIP villas. Speaking of which …

'As we approach through crystalline waters – rockstar-like, by speedboat – this mystical island unveils itself. Our butler greets us and leads us to a secluded beach house, surrounded by perfect white sand. It's love at first sight.'

HANNAH LOHAN, INTERIORS ACE

THE FINER DETAILS

BEDTIME

One-Bedroom Beach House Scan the horizon for dolphins from the comfort of this ocean-spying villa, which is a gleeful hop-and-a-skip from the beach. The private deck spills onto brown-sugar sand; its heated plunge pool gives the lapping waves a run for their money. Continue the watery adventures in the bathroom, where you'll find a generous bathtub, a rain shower and – best of all – a shower garden, where you can get as naked as peeled prawns, with nary an observer. (Call upon the stash of Como Shambhala Invigorate bath products.) There's also a spacious living room with a dining area and kitchenette, a screened-in conservatory and a bedroom befitting Neptune. The styling is as soothing to the eyes as aloe vera is to the skin: a union of wood and white that lets the giddy-blue seas and skies sing the high notes.

WORTH GETTING OUT OF BED FOR

Take part in a free open-air yoga or pilates session, get to know the hotel's mile-long private beach, and/or cool off in the shimmering infinity pool, fringed by greenery and overlooking bobbing boats. Stage a tennis, pool or ping-pong tournament if you're feeling lively; unwind with incredible ayurvedic and aromatherapy spa treatments if you're not. They say that the most important romance is the one you have with yourself, so book a session with Como's 'intuitive counsellor' for some semi-psychic guidance. Private-island pursuits on offer here include beach-lazing and scuba-diving (one of the world's top-ten scuba sites is close by). Head to the pilates cottage, conquer the running trail, sit submerged in the his 'n' hers Jacuzzis, or browse your in-room spa menu and deliberate over treatments for the morrow.

FOOD AND DRINK

Quench your thirst with the Lemon Cay Cocktail, Como's grown-up take on lemonade: a sherbet-y citrus collision of lime, lemon, vodka and triple sec. There are two watering holes – one by the poolside Lotus restaurant (where light Caribbean lunches and South East Asian fusion dinners are served); the other by the more formal, octagonal Terrace, which has an Italian-leaning Mediterranean menu. Book an unforgettable feast for two in the candlelit Tiki Hut, which overlooks the whispering waves from its privileged position. Local specialities include deliciously tender lionfish; by eating it you're doing a service to the long-suffering juvenile marine life it likes to terrorize. Conch ceviche and its zingy dressing is addictively good; the local lobster tail, slathered in garlicky lemon butter, also merits mention.

DRESS CODE

Go a little *Pirates of the Caribbean*: open-necked shirts, gypsy jewelry and a few spare gold doubloons (handy for rum sessions).

'The styling is as soothing to the eyes as aloe vera is to the skin: a union of wood and white that lets the giddy-blue seas and skies sing the high notes.'

LANGUEDOC-ROUSSILLON FRANCE

The living isn't just easy in Languedoc-Roussillon, a colour-packed coastal region in France's sultry south – it's deliciously languorous. Come for the sparkling wine, medieval Montpellier and the wild horses and flamingos of the Camargue; stay for a certain secret garden …

Taken as the locals sipped their lunchtime picpoul

Jardins Secrets

LANGUEDOC-ROUSSILLON, FRANCE

STYLE GARDENERS' WORLD
SETTING ROMAN NÎMES

Forget pulling rabbits from a hat: Jardins Secrets' magic trick is much more memorable. Behind high walls, a nondescript door and an unremarkable gate, a blush-pink 18th-century former coach house with 14 romantic rooms and a bloomin' lovely garden awaits. This languid Languedoc love nest – filled with canopied beds, sumptuous silks and antique baths – doesn't stint on style. Unlike the decor, service takes a less-is-more approach to delicious effect. There's no formal check-in, and it's the kind of place where your favourite newspaper might appear, unasked for, next to your pastries and coffee in the morning, or charcuterie and aperitifs might materialize, unsummoned, by night. Beyond your boudoir, Nîmes has had centuries to perfect its seduction: expect to be bowled over by the city's relics and ruins, which hark back to the glory days of the Roman Empire.

'You find it, you ring, the door opens and you enter a miniature Garden of Eden, with banana plants, olive trees, deck chairs and a pool. In the heart of Nîmes, it's a wonderful surprise.'

PHILIPPE TRÉTIACK, *HOMME DE MOTS*

THE FINER DETAILS

BEDTIME

Suite Edith You'll find provocative Edith tucked away in a cloister, with papal-red walls, lofty ceilings and a canopied bed that hints at anything but monkish behaviour (the ornate candlesticks and flickering light add to the blushing-priest effect). Large windows overlook the hotel's leafy-green headline act; be sure to spend some time in the suite's lavish bathroom, too, gazing in slack-jawed, wide-eyed appreciation at the orientalist mural that sprawls above the tub. Ablutions successfully completed, slip on the plush bathrobe and slippers, and snuggle up on the deliciously squashy, antique-style sofa to plan the day's adventures – outside of the bedroom or otherwise.

WORTH GETTING OUT OF BED FOR

Begin with what's right by your bedroom: those gorgeous gardens, planted with olive trees, bougainvillea and giant palms. Disrobe for the hotel's Source des Secrets spa and hammam; have a Chinese, Japanese or ayurvedic massage beside the peaceful plunge pool. Nîmes is an architectural treasure trove: visit its amphitheatre, the Maison Carrée temple and the awesome (in the trad sense) Pont du Gard, a short drive out of town. This famed triple-decker aqueduct was built by the Romans to deliver water from Uzès through the hills of the Uzège to Nîmes. You're within easy reach of some of the region's most fascinating towns, including the former papal seat Avignon, alluring Arles and Uzès, an attractive Roman town with a 15th-century Capuchin chapel. For outdoors adventures, go hiking in the Cévennes mountains or wander around Les Halles, the local food market: nibble fat Picholine olives, dig into punchy *pélardon* and admire succulent sea bream, fished while you were in the land of Nod.

FOOD AND DRINK

Adorning bedsheets and bathtubs can be hungry work, but never fear: the obliging staff will bring plates of charcuterie and cheese to your passion-hued boudoir. Breakfast is the only meal served in the hotel's pretty restaurant, but it's an indulgent cake-and-confiture bonanza. For more *jardin* hijinks come dinnertime, head to pretty, bistro-style Jardin d'Hadrien, on Rue Enclos Rey, which serves toothsome local beef and lamb dishes in its shaded garden. (Don't go home without trying the local speciality, *brandade de morue*: creamy salt cod, flavoured with olive oil.)

DRESS CODE

Make like Marie Antoinette: model ruffles, a froth of lace, a dash of velvet, deep-berry hues and an irresponsibly seductive scent. Pack your favourite pair of jeans, too: the workers' favourite fabric started life here as *serge de Nîmes*.

'This languid Languedoc love nest – filled with canopied beds, sumptuous silks and antique baths – doesn't stint on style.'

PROVENCE FRANCE

Carpeted with vivid amethyst lavender fields and blessed
with such sparkling coastal calling cards as the Côte d'Azur,
Provence's green and gold beauty has prompted a roll-call
of artists to lift their brushes, from Cézanne to Picasso.

Captured on a winter's morning with clear-as-glass skies

Villa La Coste

PROVENCE, FRANCE

STYLE ART-EN-PROVENCE
SETTING CÉZANNE'S SCENERY

Art isn't just the icing on the cake at Villa La Coste – it's the hotel's raison d'être (Cézanne grew up in these picturesque parts, after all). Boundary-pushing works by Tracey Emin and Louise Bourgeois bedeck boudoirs and communal areas; architecture comes courtesy of equally towering talent: Frank Gehry, Renzo Piano and Norman Foster, to name a few. There are plenty of soft touches to counteract the villa's shark-sleek lines, knife-edge angles and mod-minimalist appeal: impeccable service and indulgent treatments in the hushed rose and amber-scented spa, for example. More treats await in the excellent Louison restaurant, and an additional reason to raise a glass to this hotel is its wonderful wine, made on-site by Château La Coste. *Santé*!

'After dinner, a substantial amount of time was spent in our vast marble bathtub listening to Django Reinhardt and drinking more rosé. All in all, it was a perfect way to spend our first night.'

ZOË ZIMMER, GRAPHIC ARTIST

THE FINER DETAILS

BEDTIME

Pool Villa Suite This swish suite lets the Luberon valley views do the talking – and they speak volumes. Floor-to-ceiling windows open onto a spacious terrace with a scenery-surveying dining area, sun loungers and vineyard vistas; the private plunge pool beckons temptingly on hot summer afternoons. Back inside, art gallery-white walls and covetable mid-century furniture keep the style stakes lofty, and the marble-clad bathroom stars a generous tub, twin marble sinks and a walk-in rainfall shower (there's even a nifty hi-tech Japanese loo).

WORTH GETTING OUT OF BED FOR

Perhaps you're an untapped Van Gogh? Find out by packing paints and an easel and heading to the scenic Luberon Regional Nature Park, a majestic, UNESCO-listed nature reserve set in the rugged Montagne du Lubéron. Or make your way to the Calanques National Park, a 20-km (12-mile) stretch of coastline famed for its dramatic white cliffs. Hidden in between are long inlets of clear emerald water (did someone say 'wild swimming'?). For an art gallery unlike any other – aside from your new home-from-home – take a trip to the Alpilles to see the Carrières de Lumières. This former bauxite quarry contains enormous halls submerged up to 60 m (197 ft) deep beneath the mountain; its walls 'painted' with super-sized artworks, thanks to high-powered projectors. Finally, get filthy at the spa: couples can be slathered in warm medicinal muds, redolent of rose and amber, and buttery apricot and olive body balms. Stake out the double treatment room, which has a romantic private garden.

FOOD AND DRINK

Acclaimed chef Gérald Passédat rustles up edible art at the Louison restaurant, harnessing hero Provençal flavours for his dishes, which champion produce from the kitchen garden and local markets. It's an impressive setting: a glittering, glass-walled building suspended above water, with two chrome-covered figures dangling from the ceiling. Light streams in from all sides (all the better for admiring what's on your plate). For more casual offerings, pay a visit to the Salon, which serves elevated regional cuisine in your choice of settings: the living room, library, gallery or garden, perhaps? (You can also order foie gras on chutney toast, saffron risotto and more to be brought to your room between meals.) Art is one reason to hit the marble bar, where works by Damien Hirst and Sean Scully add visual fireworks to a bright-white space; Château La Coste's excellent wine is another.

DRESS CODE

Local hero Cézanne favoured vivid natural hues; you should, too. Honour the hotel's enviable art stash by embracing avant-garde garms a-go-go.

'Art is one reason to hit the marble bar, where works by Damien Hirst and Sean Scully add visual fireworks to a bright-white space; Château La Coste's excellent wine is another.'

SANTA CATARINA BRAZIL

This beach-graced state in southern Brazil has Mother
Nature to thank for its jagged mountains and eye-popping
560 km (350 mile)-long coastline; and an influx of German
immigrants to thank for its excellent beer, Alpine architecture
and blue-eyed, flaxen-haired locals.

*Shot as the island relaxed after March's
kaleidoscopic carnival*

Ponta dos Ganchos

SANTA CATARINA, BRAZIL

STYLE JUNGLIST MASSIVE

SETTING PRIVATE PENINSULA PERFECTION

You're not short of aphrodisiacs at Ponta dos Ganchos on Brazil's Emerald Coast: Santa Catarina's waters are abrim with love-boosting bivalves, after all. Not that you have to visit the local oyster farms to get in the mood, mind: this heavenly hideaway's private island and billion-dollar-baby bungalows will quicken your pulse and weaken your knees. This particular version of paradise comes with clay tennis courts, a games room, cinema and spa. Best of all, perhaps, are the stunning sea views, which you can admire at every turn, since the hotel is hugged by waves. (NB: If you fancy dropping in by chopper, jot down these coordinates: 27°18' 26 S 048° 33'06 W.)

'That's it, I decide. I never need anything more than oyster *moqueca*, cold caipirinhas, bossa nova records and this bay-view bath. Come check-out, life seems desperately unfair.'

RICHARD MACKICHAN, EDITOR, MR & MRS SMITH

THE FINER DETAILS

BEDTIME

Especial Esmeralda Bungalow There are
bungalows – and then there are *bungalows*.
Ponta dos Ganchos's Especial Esmeralda
Bungalow belongs in the latter category. Let's
start with the wooden deck and its tropical
garden and glittering infinity pool, which
appears to drop down into the ocean and
greenery below. Then there's the bathroom and
its giant, sea-surveying bathtub, perched by the
floor-to-ceiling windows; a tempting daybed
and view-maximizing loungers hint at deliciously
idle hours. The open-plan bedroom continues the
seascape-seduction. Bed down here and you'll
feel at the very top of the A-list: the living room
has a fireplace, a home cinema, a private wine
cellar and a Jacuzzi and sauna set in an ocean-
facing bay window with a glass roof.

WORTH GETTING OUT OF BED FOR

Explore nature trails, hike to the beach (keep your
eyes peeled for migrating whales between June and
November) and have spa treatments by the water's
edge. Don't be alarmed if the heavens open, just
take your pick from 300-plus movies to screen at
the cinema or swing by the kitchens for a culinary
masterclass. Go a little further afield and net some
oysters on a boat trip with a local fisherman. Fancy
sipping ice-cold German beer in your tropical
surroundings? The Eisenbahn microbrewery is
two hours away. Beach bunnies should pack towels
and a chef-prepped picnic for blissful Praia do
Rosa, Lagoinha do Leste, Lagoa da Conceição and
Campeche Island; keen surfers will fall for Guarda
do Embaú's challenging breaks.

FOOD AND DRINK

Breakfast like Brazilian champions by downing
fruit shots and tucking into *bolinho de chuva*
(cinnamon-dusted doughnuts). Seafood is a
natural highlight; the hotel does a fine line in beach
barbecues starring just-caught fish – its oyster
moqueca is also applaudable. Wine-lovers will
be in grapey heaven: there are over 240 choices to
sip through. Don't go home without ordering at
least one Hook cocktail, made with cachaça and
physalis plucked from the Amazon.

DRESS CODE

Model light, white linen and a grateful grin.
(You'll be treated to box-fresh Havaianas on
arrival, so leave your old battered ones behind.)

'Best of all, perhaps, are the
stunning sea views, which you can
admire at every turn, since the hotel
is hugged by waves.'

PILLOW TALK

These people deserve enormous thanks and a very, very long lie-in: Polly Brown for the peerless pictures; Sarah Jappy for her winning wordsmithery; Jason Badrock for design and layouts; Richard MacKichan for endurance editing; Helen Bailey for press-tempting and project-managing; Hannah Jones for travel-planning *par excellence*; the Thames & Hudson team for turning our idea into a reality; James Lohan for having the idea to do something fun in print again to celebrate our 15th birthday; and Tamara Lohan for honing our shortlist of favourites.

Suite-sized thanks to all our reviewers for giving us the inside track (with notable mentions to Laura Snapes, Matthew Malin, Henrietta Thompson and David Weiner for going above and beyond) and every hotel featured for being so accommodating and, well, sexy.

To our team of curators – Elise Tagatac, Georgia Lee, Carla Melmoth, Aimee Hodgkin, Marion Barrère, Emily Cunningham, Becca Williams, Jenny Mouyon, Charlotte Heyman, Abigail Gill and Annalyn Hood – thanks for never settling for anything less than perfection. And to all our members around the world, we couldn't have done any of this without you, so huge and heartfelt thanks for your loyalty over the years.

Thanks also, and raised glasses, to Rosie Maguire at We Folk, contract queen Natasha Shafi, CEO Ed Orr and the entire Mr & Mrs Smith team, and hotel lovers everywhere.

MR & MRS SMITH

Chief creative officer James Lohan
Writer Sarah Jappy
Editor Richard MacKichan
Design Badrock Design
Press Helen Bailey

All information correct at the time of going to print. Mr & Mrs Smith apologizes for any errors, inaccuracies or omissions.

ADDRESSES TO IMPRESS

INDEX

DO NOT
DISTURB

On the cover and page 198: Uxua Casa Hotel & Spa, Bahia, Brazil.
Page 2: Annandale, Pigeon Bay, New Zealand.
Page 4: Le Roch Hotel & Spa, Paris, France.
Page 6: The Williamsburg Hotel, New York, United States.
Pages 288 and 295: the Beaumont Hotel, London, United Kingdom.

First published in the United Kingdom in 2018
by Thames & Hudson Ltd, 181a High Holborn,
London WC1V 7QX

Mr & Mrs Smith Presents the World's Sexiest Bedrooms
© 2018 Thames & Hudson Ltd, London

Text © 2018 Smith Global Ltd
All photographs © 2018 Polly Brown, with the exception of the
photographs on pages 116 and 117 (top) © 2018 Awasi Patagonia.

Designed by Badrock Design

British Library Cataloguing-in-Publication Data
A catalogue record for this book is available from the British Library

ISBN 978-0-500-02178-1

Printed and bound in China by C & C Offset Printing Co. Ltd

To find out about all our publications, please visit
www.thamesandhudson.com. There you can subscribe
to our e-newsletter, browse or download our current
catalogue, and buy any titles that are in print.